Economic Outlook for Southeast Asia, China and India 2018 - Update

PROMOTING OPPORTUNITIES IN E-COMMERCE

This work is published under the responsibility of the Secretary-General of the OECD. The opinions expressed and arguments employed herein do not necessarily reflect the official views of the member countries of the OECD or its Development Centre.

This document, as well as any data and any map included herein, are without prejudice to the status of or sovereignty over any territory, to the delimitation of international frontiers and boundaries and to the name of any territory, city or area.

Please cite this publication as:
OECD (2018), *Economic Outlook for Southeast Asia, China and India 2018 - Update: Promoting Opportunities in E-commerce*, OECD Publishing, Paris.
https://doi.org/10.1787/9789264302990-en

ISBN 978-92-64-30298-3 (print)
ISBN 978-92-64-30299-0 (PDF)

Photo credits: Cover © OECD 2018

Corrigenda to OECD publications may be found on line at: *www.oecd.org/about/publishing/corrigenda.htm*.
© OECD 2018

You can copy, download or print OECD content for your own use, and you can include excerpts from OECD publications, databases and multimedia products in your own documents, presentations, blogs, websites and teaching materials, provided that suitable acknowledgment of the source and copyright owner(s) is given. All requests for public or commercial use and translation rights should be submitted to *rights@oecd.org*. Requests for permission to photocopy portions of this material for public or commercial use shall be addressed directly to the Copyright Clearance Center (CCC) at *info@copyright.com* or the Centre francais d'exploitation du droit de copie (CFC) at *contact@cfcopies.com*.

Foreword

The *Economic Outlook for Southeast Asia, China and India - Update* is released following the main report of the *Outlook*, to ensure that its data, projections and policy discussions remain up-to-date and relevant. Both reports focus on the economic conditions of the Association of Southeast Asian Nations (ASEAN) member countries (Brunei Darussalam, Cambodia, Indonesia, Lao PDR, Malaysia, Myanmar, the Philippines, Singapore, Thailand and Viet Nam) and two large economies in the region, China and India. This publication evolved from the *Southeast Asian Economic Outlook*. Beginning with the first release of the *Update to the Outlook* in June 2016, the *Outlook* has become a biannual publication. The 2018 *Update* is the first edition to be released as an independent publication.

The *Outlook* was initially proposed at an informal reflection group on Southeast Asia in 2008 as a follow-up of the Council Meeting at Ministerial level (MCM) in 2007 and was accepted by ministers/senior officials from ASEAN countries at the occasion of the 2nd OECD-Southeast Asia Regional Forum in Bangkok in 2009. The *Outlook* project was officially launched in 2010 and each edition is regularly presented at the occasion of the ASEAN/East Asia Summit. It was included in the OECD's Southeast Asia Regional Programme (SEARP) at the Steering Group Meeting in Jakarta, Indonesia in March 2015, with its role of providing a horizontal view of activities, identifying emerging trends in the region and providing a backbone for the different streams of the Programme confirmed at the 2015 MCM. The *Outlook* serves as a strategic foresight and policy dialogue tool for the SEARP and includes summaries of recent developments in the region on issues related to the Programme's six Regional Policy Networks and three Initiatives.

This edition of the *Update* is comprised of two main parts: a regional economic monitor and a thematic focus specific to this year's reports. The 2018 edition of the *Update* focuses on the opportunities and challenges of cross-border e-commerce in Emerging Asia. The region has seen rapid growth in e-commerce in recent years and is expected to account for a large share of the global market in the future. Ensuring that the potential benefits of this trend are realised will require governments to make improvements to connectivity, skills, digital security and consumer protection, and regional and international co-operation.

The OECD Development Centre is committed to working alongside governments of developing and emerging economies and regional actors to identify key areas of intervention in order to address these challenges. The Centre enjoys the full membership of three Southeast Asian countries, namely Indonesia, Thailand and Viet Nam, as well as India and China. This project has also benefitted from the generous support of other Emerging Asian countries.

Like other regional economic outlooks produced by the OECD Development Centre, this report was prepared in collaboration with regional partners; UNESCAP and the Economic Research Institute for ASEAN and East Asia (ERIA) contributed to the 2018 edition. The *Update* also benefited from discussions with the ASEAN Secretariat. The OECD is committed to supporting Asian countries in their efforts to promote economic and social well-being through rigorous analysis, peer learning and best practices.

Acknowledgements

The *Economic Outlook for Southeast Asia, China and India 2018 - Update: Promoting Opportunities in E-commerce* was prepared by the Asia Desk of the OECD Development Centre, in co-operation with United Nations Economic and Social Commission for Asia and the Pacific (UNESCAP) and the Economic Research Institute for ASEAN and East Asia (ERIA). The publication also benefited from discussions with the ASEAN Secretariat.

The team was led by Kensuke Tanaka, Head of the Asia Desk and valuable guidance was provided by Mario Pezzini, Director of the OECD Development Centre as well as suggestions by Naoko Ueda, Deputy Director. This volume was drafted by a team composed of Kensuke Tanaka, Prasiwi Ibrahim, Derek Carnegie, Ryan Jacildo, Juita Mohamad, Jingjing Xia, Lurong Chen, and Masato Abe. Jingjing Xia also contributed to statistical work related to this publication and Jihyeon Kim, Jaewon Kim, Fiona Valente and Yuanita Suhud provided useful inputs. Elizabeth Nash, Delphine Grandrieux, Studio Pykha and Aida Buendia turned the manuscript into the publication.

The Outlook's 2018 Update benefited from discussions with OECD Delegations at the Outlook Consultation Group (OCG) meetings in March, September, November 2017 and February 2018 in Paris, led by co-chairs of this consultation group, Ambassador Jong-Won Yoon, Ambassador Ma. Theresa Lazaro and Counsellor Jürg Schneider, together with Ambassador Pierre Duquesne. The Outlook also benefited from discussion with experts in the region and other international organisations. The authors are grateful to Rintaro Tamaki, former Deputy Secretary-General of the OECD, Chang Junhong, Director of AMRO, Naoyuki Yoshino, Dean of the ADBI, Hidetoshi Nishimura, President of ERIA, as well as Aladdin Rillo, Izuru Kobayashi, Fukunari Kimura, Ng Chuin Hwei, Yumiko Murakami, Atsushi Higuchi and Joseph E. Zveglich, Jr. The full Outlook 2018 report was presented at the occasion of the ASEAN/East Asia Summit in Manila, the Philippines in November 2017.

Support from OECD delegations and embassies of Asian countries in Paris, in particular, Ambassador Hiroshi Oe, Ambassador Sihasak Phuangketkeow, Ambassador Nguyen Thiep, Rapunzel Acop, Rudjimin, Fajar Harijo, Takuma Kajita, Masahiro Katsuno, Venugopal Menon, Tze Shen Ong, Junhee Lee, Hye Ryoung Song, Karina Ratnamurti, Sarvjeet Soodan, Houmphanh Soukprasith, Sisouphanh Keobandavong, Soveasna Sun, Sasilada Kusump, Sirichada Thongtan, Sean Tan, Teddy Low, Phuong Nguyen, Nguyen Thanh Thao, Zaidah Shahminan, Thyra Chheang, Thein Min Htun, Shwe Yi Phyo, Bin Zhang, Bo Chen, Sining Zhao, Hans Siriban, Froilan Emil Pamintuan, Seinn Lei Tun, Tran Phan Linh, Canh Cuong Nguyen, Sovanra Nong, Rakesh K. Sharma, and Tomoki Watanabe, is gratefully acknowledged.

Last but not least, the OECD Development Centre would like to acknowledge gratefully the financial support received from the governments of Japan, Korea and Switzerland.

Table of contents

Executive summary 11

Overview 13

Chapter 1. Macroeconomic assessments and economic outlook for Emerging Asia 23
    Introduction 24
    Overview and main findings 26
    Other key points of the economic outlook and assessment 28
    Recent macroeconomic developments and near-term prospects 29
    Headline inflation is firming up in some countries in the region 45
    Central banks have started to raise policy rates but are using other tools to maintain liquidity 48
    Current account balances remain moderate, except for those of oil exporters 50
    FDI inflows remain strong for most Emerging Asian countries 52
    Capital markets adjust to tighter liquidity and the downward pull on asset prices 54
    Banking systems are generally sound as NPL-related pressures recede 58
    Fiscal consolidation sentiment mounts among governments in the region 61
    Challenges for robust growth 66
    Notes 76
    References 77

Chapter 2. Emerging Asia in the era of cross-border e-commerce 79
    Introduction 80
    Cross-border e-commerce trends and outlook 80
    Factors affecting the growth of cross-border e-commerce 83
    Policy challenges and conclusion 94
    Notes 100
    References 100

Statistical annex 103

Tables

    1.1 Real GDP growth in ASEAN, China and India 26
    1.2 Recent real GDP growth in ASEAN, China and India 27
    1.3 Main features of TRAIN 1A 66
    1.4 Summary of recent central bank policy-rate changes in Emerging Asia 67
    1.5 Correlation of Emerging Asia benchmarket bond yields with US benchmark bond yields 68
    1.6 Recent capital expenditure in selected Emerging Asian countries 72
    1.7 Status of ADB sovereign projects in Emerging Asia, 2013-17 73
    1.8 Non-tariff measures recorded in 2015 for ASEAN members 76
    2.1 Forms of e-commerce and other Internet applications 80
    2.2 Firm-level technology adoption in ASEAN, China and India, 2007-17 85
    2.3 IPv4 addresses by broadband connection speed in Emerging Asia, Q1 2017 86
    2.4 Infrastructure quality in Emerging Asia 89
    2.5 E-commerce laws in ASEAN Member States, 2013 92
    A.1 Real GDP growth of Southeast Asia, China and India 103
    A.2 Current account balances of Southeast Asia, China and India 103
    A.3 General government financial balances of Southeast Asia, China and India ... 104

TABLE OF CONTENTS

Figures
1.1 Real GDP growth of Southeast Asia, China and India 25
1.2 Contribution to real GDP growth in ASEAN-5 countries, 2015-17 29
1.3 Consumer confidence indices in selected ASEAN countries, 2016-18 30
1.4 Value of goods exports from ASEAN-5 countries, 2017-18 31
1.5 Industrial Production Indices in ASEAN-5 countries, 2017-18 34
1.6 Tourist arrivals in ASEAN-5 countries, 2017-18 34
1.7 Contribution to real GDP growth in Brunei Darussalam and Singapore, 2015-17 35
1.8 Value of goods exports from Brunei Darussalam and Singapore, 2017-18 36
1.9 Contribution to real GDP growth in Cambodia, Lao PDR and Myanmar, 2015-17 37
1.10 Value of goods exports from Cambodia, Lao PDR and Myanmar, 2016-18 38
1.11 OECD FDI Regulatory Restrictiveness Index scores in Emerging Asia, 2017 39
1.12 Contribution to real GDP growth in China and India, 2015-17 41
1.13 Value of goods exports from China and India, 2017-18 42
1.14 Purchasing Managers' Indices in China and India, 2016-18 42
1.15 Corporate debt to GDP in China and G7 economies, Q1 2006 – Q4 2017 43
1.16 Household debt to GDP in China and G7 economies, Q1 2006 – Q4 2017 43
1.17 Consumer confidence indices in China and India, 2016-18 44
1.18 Inflation in Emerging Asia, 2017-18 46
1.19 Evolution of inflation and benchmark interest rates 49
1.20 Current account balances of Emerging Asian countries, 2016-19 51
1.21 Foreign direct investment in Emerging Asian countries, 2014-18 53
1.22 Benchmark bond yield and term spreads in the United States and Emerging Asia, 2012-18 ... 55
1.23 Portfolio and other investment inflows in Emerging Asian countries, 2014-18 56
1.24 Credit Default Swap (5-year senior) in ASEAN-5 and China, 2015-18 56
1.25 Equity market returns in Emerging Asia, 2016-18 57
1.26 Nominal effective exchange rate in Emerging Asia, 2017-18 58
1.27 Bank lending in Emerging Asian countries, 2016-18 59
1.28 Non-performing loans ratio in Emerging Asian countries, 2017-18 60
1.29 General government financial balance in Emerging Asia, 2018-19 62
1.30 Tax reform packages in Indonesia 65
1.31 Estimated infrastructure investment and needs in Emerging Asian countries, 2017 70
1.32 Public-private partnership (PPP) projects in Emerging Asia by type, 2013-17 74
2.1 ICT use in B2B and B2C transactions, 2014-16 81
2.2 E-commerce market revenue, 2015-21 81
2.3 E-commerce users, 2015-21 82
2.4 Compound annual growth rate of B2C e-commerce sales, 2016-21 82
2.5 E-Participation Index, 2012 and 2016 83
2.6 Internet users as a percentage of population, 2000-16 84
2.7 Proportion of businesses receiving orders over the Internet by size, 2014 85
2.8 Number and growth of mobile telephone subscriptions, 2000-15 87
2.9 Internet prices in Emerging Asia, 2015 88
2.10 Internet scams in selected Emerging Asian countries, 2016 93
2.11 Students with at least one computer at home, 2009-12 97

Boxes

1.1 Malaysia is undergoing restructuring with the new Pakatan Harapan government 31
1.2 Policies supporting foreign direct investment in Cambodia, Lao PDR and Myanmar 39
1.3 Changing trends in China's debt 43
1.4 Relative valuation of the stock price of companies in Emerging Asia 57
1.5 Recent tax reforms in some Emerging Asian countries 64
2.1 E-government in Emerging Asia 83
2.2 Mobile Internet and e-commerce 87
2.3 Innovation for financial inclusion 90
2.4 Electronic authentication 93
2.5 E-commerce in national development plans 94

Executive summary

The *Economic Outlook for Southeast Asia, China and India - Update* is released following the main report of the *Outlook*, to ensure that its data, projections and policy discussions remain up-to-date and relevant. The 2018 edition of the *Update* covers two main topics on Emerging Asia: the near-term regional economic outlook in 2018 and 2019 (Chapter 1) and the opportunities and challenges for the region posed by the rapid growth of cross-border e-commerce (Chapter 2).

Economic outlook for 2018 and 2019

Real GDP growth in Emerging Asia (Southeast Asia, China and India) remained robust in 2017, averaging 6.5%, following growth of 6.4% in 2016. Southeast Asia grew substantially faster in 2017 than in the previous year, with most of the ASEAN economies posting higher growth rates. Growth in China also improved, while it dipped slightly in India. Emerging Asia is expected to grow by 6.6% in 2018 and 6.5% in 2019, on the basis of generally robust consumption and investment. The ten ASEAN economies are expected to see average growth of 5.3% in both 2018 and 2019, with the highest rates of growth in the CLM countries (Cambodia, Lao PDR and Myanmar), Viet Nam and the Philippines. Growth in China is projected to slip somewhat to 6.7% in 2018 and 6.4% in 2019, and to improve in India to 7.4% in 2018 and 7.5% in 2019.

Overall, the external positions of the Emerging Asian economies have remained stable thus far; current account balances have improved in a number of economies in the region and FDI data show an even more encouraging picture. Policy rates in the region have been increased, mainly in response to increases in inflationary pressure and weakness in local currency of some economies, though monetary authorities have also used reserve requirements to maintain liquidity. Meanwhile, a number of large economies in the region are consolidating their budgetary positions.

Challenges to this outlook and the maintenance of robust rates of growth in the region remain, related to rising interest rates, infrastructure investment and trade. Rising interest rates in advanced economies could have negative effects on capital flows and domestic demand in the region. Planned infrastructure projects could help to support growth in the near term, but obstacles in the timely implementation of these projects pose negative risks to growth. Continued regional integration will be challenged and possibly made more important by rising protectionist sentiments globally.

Cross-border e-commerce

While it remains smaller than other forms of commerce, global cross-border business-to-business (B2B) and business-to-consumer (B2C) e-commerce is expanding rapidly. The Emerging Asian economies are already important players in these markets and are expected to help drive future growth. From 2015 to 2021, the region's total B2C e-commerce market revenue is expected to increase from about USD 320 billion (US dollars) to more than USD 900 billion. China's market will contribute more than 90% of this growth; the country's share in the global e-commerce market will increase from about 30% in 2015 to nearly 40% in 2021. India and ASEAN will increase their combined weight in the global market from 2.5% to 4%. Emerging Asia will also contribute a disproportionately large share of global Internet and e-commerce users.

These prospects for continued growth are the result of generally favourable conditions in the region, though challenges also remain in ensuring that the potential benefits of e-commerce are realised. The use of information and communication technology (ICT) by individuals and firms is spreading. ICT infrastructure, while still underdeveloped in some countries and areas, has also grown. Mobile technologies have proven to be particularly useful in expanding Internet access. More work could be done in addressing the challenges for transport and logistics systems posed by growing cross-border e-commerce. While e-payment systems remain underdeveloped, solutions are emerging in the region. Across much of Emerging Asia, the legal and regulatory frameworks needed to foster the growth of e-commerce have been established, though gaps remain in this area as well and solutions are needed that encourage fair competition and build trust between participants.

Governments in the region can help to promote the development of cross-border e-commerce. It will be important to improve connectivity, though investment in transportation and ICT infrastructure and the implementation of policies supporting efficient logistics and other supporting systems. The region's human resource potential could be built upon in developing the skills needed for further growth in e-commerce. Concerns about digital security and consumer should be addressed. Finally, regional and international co-operation should be pursued in regulatory harmonisation and the minimisation of costs in cross-border transactions, while promoting other policy goals.

Overview

Chapter 1: Macroeconomic assessment and economic outlook for Emerging Asia

Economic growth in Emerging Asia – Southeast Asia, China and India – remains robust: it expanded by 6.5% in 2017, slightly stronger than in 2016. Most countries of the Association of Southeast Asian Nations (ASEAN) grew substantially faster in 2017 than in the previous year (ASEAN's member states are Brunei Darussalam, Cambodia, Indonesia, Lao PDR, Malaysia, Myanmar, the Philippines, Singapore, Thailand and Viet Nam). China's growth rate surpassed the government's target, while India managed to navigate quite well the growth obstacles tied to lagged demonetisation effects and the sales tax reform. Strong economic growth in Emerging Asia is projected to continue in 2018 and 2019. This prognosis is backed by generally robust domestic demand. Central banks have started raising their policy rates, largely on concerns related to inflation and exchange rates, but they have used other instruments to keep market liquidity ample. External demand is likely to be relatively reserved, in light of new tariff measures of some economies.

Optimism in capital markets has softened, but Emerging Asian economies' external positions have remained mostly stable so far. Current account balances have improved in a number of the region's economies, while foreign direct investment (FDI) inflows show an even more encouraging picture. Inflation has picked up in some countries, and the build up of price pressures has prompted some central banks to take a more proactive stance, although the prevailing rates are still within tolerance bands. Emerging Asian countries must cope with the following challenges to maintain growth: the impact of rising interest rates in advanced economies, in particular the United States, the implementation of planned infrastructure projects and the acceleration of regional integration amidst rising protectionism.

Overview and main findings: The economic outlook for 2018-19

Emerging Asia's aggregate real gross domestic product (GDP) growth is expected to firm up to 6.6% in 2018 and 6.5% in 2019 (Table 1). Southeast Asia's economy is estimated to grow at a steady pace of 5.3% in the next two years on the back of resilient domestic demand in many countries, though trade prospects are uncertain. In China, GDP growth is forecast to nudge downwards in 2018 and 2019, while GDP growth in India is projected to increase during the same period.

Table 1. **Real GDP growth in ASEAN, China and India**
Annual percentage change

	2016	2017	2018	2019
ASEAN-5 countries				
Indonesia	5.0	5.1	5.3	5.4
Malaysia	4.2	5.9	5.3	5.1
Philippines	6.9	6.7	6.7	6.7
Thailand	3.3	3.9	4.0	3.9
Viet Nam	6.2	6.8	6.9	6.6
Brunei Darussalam and Singapore				
Brunei Darussalam	-2.5	1.3	1.5	2.1
Singapore	2.4	3.6	3.5	3.0
CLM countries				
Cambodia	6.9	7.0	7.0	7.0
Lao PDR	7.0	6.9	6.8	6.9
Myanmar	5.9	6.8	6.9	7.1
China and India				
China	6.7	6.9	6.7	6.4
India	7.1	6.7	7.4	7.5
Average of ASEAN-10	**4.8**	**5.3**	**5.3**	**5.3**
Average of Emerging Asia	**6.4**	**6.5**	**6.6**	**6.5**

Notes: The cut-off date for data used is 18 June 2018. ASEAN and Emerging Asia growth rates are the weighted averages of the individual economies subsumed. Cambodia and Myanmar's 2017 data are preliminary estimates. The data of India and Myanmar follow fiscal years. For Myanmar, 2018 refers to the interim six-month period from April 2018 to September 2018, while 2019 refers to the fiscal year from October 2018 to September 2019. The projections of China, India and Indonesia are based on the OECD Economic Outlook No. 103 (database).
Source: OECD Development Centre, *Medium-term Projection Framework* (MPF-2018).

ASEAN-5

- **Indonesia**'s GDP growth will marginally improve to 5.3% in 2018 and 5.4% in 2019 on promising investment trends and robust consumer-demand indicators, anchored by wage adjustments, the hosting of the Asian Games and upcoming presidential elections. GDP growth in the first quarter (Q1) of 2018 was 5.1% more or less the same pace observed in Q4 2017 (Table 2).

- **Malaysia**'s economic expansion is projected to moderate to 5.3% in 2018 and 5.1% in 2019 from 5.9% in 2017, largely in line with its average growth rate since 2010, though there are some uncertainties about the new administration's policies. The decision to review large infrastructure investment projects could dampen fixed investment growth. On the upside, private consumption indicators and exports are moving along relatively well. Data in Q1 2018 show that GDP growth has eased to 5.4% from 5.6% in the same period last year.

- The **Philippines** is estimated to replicate its 2017 GDP growth of 6.7% in 2018 and in 2019. Government spending and public investment will likely anchor economic growth, with private consumption facing some friction and exports substantially weakening. Data in Q1 2018 show that the Philippine economy expanded by 6.8%, about 30 basis points faster than in Q1 2017.

- GDP growth in **Thailand** is expected to come in at 4.0% in 2018 and 3.9% in 2019. Exports are still growing strongly, benefitting the domestic industrial sector. Private consumption indicators point to an increase in expenditures, even as the government plans to continue consolidating its fiscal position. The economy started 2018 with an encouraging 4.8% expansion in Q1 2018, up from 3.4% in Q1 2017.

- In **Viet Nam**, GDP is projected to grow by 6.9% in 2018 and 6.6% in 2019. Data in the first half (H1) of 2018 showed a GDP growth of 7.1% (7.5% in Q1 and 6.8% in Q2), up from 5.7% in H1 2017. Private consumption is expected to remain robust. However, exports and investment intake are showing signs of moderating.

Table 2. **Recent real GDP growth in ASEAN, China and India**
Quarterly, year-on-year percentage change

	Q1 2017	Q2 2017	Q3 2017	Q4 2017	Q1 2018
ASEAN-5 countries					
Indonesia	5.0	5.0	5.1	5.2	5.1
Malaysia	5.6	5.8	6.2	5.9	5.4
Philippines	6.5	6.6	7.2	6.5	6.8
Thailand	3.4	3.9	4.3	4.0	4.8
Viet Nam	5.2	6.3	7.5	7.7	7.5
Brunei Darussalam and Singapore					
Brunei Darussalam	-1.3	0.2	1.3	5.2	—
Singapore	2.5	2.8	5.5	3.6	4.4
China and India					
China	6.9	6.9	6.8	6.8	6.8
India	5.6	6.3	7.0	7.7	—

Notes: The cut-off date for data used is 18 June 2018. Quarterly data are not available for Cambodia, Lao PDR and Myanmar. Data for India follow fiscal years.
Source: OECD Development Centre based on CEIC and national sources.

Brunei Darussalam and Singapore

- **Brunei Darussalam**'s economy grew in 2017 for the first time since 2012, and it is expected to expand by 1.5% in 2018 and by 2.1% in 2019. Higher global oil prices should bode well for exports, fiscal space and the domestic labour market.
- In **Singapore**, the economy is expected to grow by 3.5% in 2018 and by 3.0% in 2019. Data in Q1 2018 show an economic expansion rate of 4.4%, up from 2.5% in Q1 2017, largely on the strength of exports. However, offshore shipments, which underpin a large portion of domestic industrial production and some services segments, could face stiff headwinds due to new tariff schedules in some large economies. The realisation of planned large transportation infrastructure projects should limit downside risks.

CLM countries

- In **Cambodia**, GDP is expected to grow annually by 7.0% in 2018 and 2019. Construction activities will help keep domestic consumption resilient. Exports have also grown sizeably so far in 2018, although substantial risks are looming.
- In **Lao PDR**, GDP growth is estimated to settle at 6.8% in 2018 and to rise to 6.9% in 2019. The expansion of overseas electricity deals and the strong influx of foreign direct investment are a boon to the country's growth prospects in the near term.
- In **Myanmar**, the economy is expected to grow by about 6.9% in the interim six-month period from April 2018 to September 2018 and by 7.1% in fiscal year 2019 (October 2018 to September 2019). Consumption will likely remain buoyant on wage adjustments. The economy should also benefit from infrastructure projects that have been pushed forward to clear the pipeline.

China and India

- **China's** GDP growth is projected to moderate to 6.7% in 2018 and to 6.4% in 2019. Household consumption is expected to maintain a relatively steady expansion rate on the back of robust real disposable income growth. A potential source of downside risk is escalating trade tensions, leading to tariffs on an increasing number of goods. This could hurt exports and potentially spill over to investment by export-oriented firms. Recent data show that China's GDP grew by 6.8% in Q1 2018, marginally lower than the 6.9% in Q1 2017.
- Meanwhile, **India's** economic growth is poised to rise to 7.4% in 2018 and 7.5% in 2019. Private spending should benefit from rising credit growth. Improvements in revenue intake should also help the government expand spending coverage. The issues related to banks' non-performing assets will require careful attention.

Other key points of the economic outlook and assessment

- Overall, the external positions of Emerging Asian economies have remained stable so far. Current account balances have improved in a number of economies in the region. FDI data show an even more encouraging picture. Overall risk perception in financial markets in the region has risen since early 2018, although the degree of concern is still relatively limited.
- Monetary authorities in Emerging Asia have started raising policy rates, mainly on the grounds of rising inflation and weakening of some local currencies. However, they have also used the mandated reserve requirement ratio for banks to keep the system liquid, presumably to isolate the direct monetary policy impact on exchange rates, inflation and domestic credit flows. Headline inflation in several Emerging Asian countries has been climbing since the end of 2017, propelled partly by the rise in global oil prices and the strengthening of the US dollar. Local currencies like the Philippine peso, Indonesian rupiah and Indian rupee have depreciated this year.
- Overall, the fiscal positions of Emerging Asian economies are relatively sound. The fiscal policy direction, however, is mixed. Revenue performances (i.e. revenue-to-GDP ratio) diverged across the region from 2016 to 2017. While the revenue ratios of Cambodia, the Philippines, Singapore and Viet Nam have either improved or remained stable, the ratios of Brunei Darussalam, China, India, Indonesia, Lao PDR, Malaysia and Thailand have deteriorated.

Challenges to the outlook

Economies in the region will need to cope with several challenges to maintain robust growth. A few prominent issues highlighted in this report are:

- the impact of rising interest rates in advanced economies, in particular the United States
- the implementation of infrastructure projects
- the acceleration of regional integration amidst rising protectionism.

The impact of rising interest rates in advanced economies, in particular the United States, on Emerging Asia requires careful attention. Although the risk is benign at this point, the potential that it can trigger substantial capital outflows cannot be set aside, considering the recent broadening of domestic inflation pressures, weakening of currencies in the region and growing credit risk perception. The risk that domestic demand could be dampened because of higher domestic borrowing costs is another concern. Some central banks in the region have recently raised policy rates in response to the currency weakness and inflation build-up, which can be partly associated with the monetary policy of the United States (Table 3). Incidentally, the correlation of 1-year benchmark bond yields has also strengthened this year compared with previous periods. With domestic interest rates rising more sternly, consumption and investment prospects could be diminished, which will consequently negatively influence trade. This may also create some complications in the ongoing efforts to resolve financial asset quality issues in some of the Emerging Asia economies.

Table 3. **Summary of recent central bank policy rate changes in Emerging Asia**

Country	Policy rate action	Primary underlying reasons
India	6 June 2018: RBI raised the policy repo rate, reverse repo rate, marginal standing facility rate and the bank rate by 25 bps each.	RBI raised rates to achieve the medium-term target of 4.0% (+/-2 percentage points) for consumer price index (CPI) inflation, which has responded strongly to the recent global oil price volatility.
Indonesia	17 May 2018: BI raised the seven-day reverse repo rate, deposit facility rate and lending facility rates by 25 bps each.	BI increased rates to maintain economic stability amid escalating global financial market risks and the global liquidity downturn. BI will continue with rupiah exchange-rate stabilisation measures, while maintaining adequate liquidity in the foreign exchange and money markets.
	30 May 2018: BI raised the seven-day reverse repo rate, deposit facility rate and lending facility rates by 25 bps each.	The rate hikes were a pre-emptive move to maintain exchange rate stability against a higher-than-expected US Federal Funds Rate increase and rising risks in the global financial market, while keeping inflation in check. BI will continue to intervene in the foreign-exchange and government-securities markets to stabilise rupiah exchange rates, adjust fair prices in the financial markets, and maintain adequate liquidity in the money and interbank swap markets.
	29 June 2018: BI raised the 7-day Reverse Repo rate, deposit facility rate and lending facility rates by 50 bps each.	The rate hikes were a pre-emptive measure to maintain the domestic financial market's competitiveness against several countries' changing monetary policies as well as high global uncertainty consistent with the framework of dual intervention policy in the foreign exchange market and government securities markets.
Malaysia	25 January 2018: BNM raised the overnight policy rate and its corresponding floor and ceiling rates by 25 bps.	BNM increased rates to normalise the degree of monetary accommodation, given the economy's reassuring strength, and to prevent the build-up of risks that could arise from protracted low interest rates.
Philippines	10 May 2018: BSP raised the overnight reverse repurchase rate, overnight lending rate and overnight deposit rate by 25 bps each.	BSP raised rates to arrest an increase in inflation expectations amid broadening inflation pressures. BSP noted that it continues to survey the domestic and global economic environment, including the potential impact of the monetary policy normalisation in advanced economies.
	20 June 2018: BSP raised overnight reverse repurchase rate, overnight lending rate and overnight deposit rate by 25 bps each.	BSP raised rates to mitigate upside risks to inflation outlook and the risk of second-round effects. BSP will remain vigilant against domestic and international developments, including excessive peso volatility, that could affect the outlook for inflation.

Source: OECD Development Centre compilation based on national central bank sources.

The extent of the effectiveness of infrastructure-project implementation can be both an upside and downside risk to economic activity. Timely and efficient implementation of infrastructure plans can be a strong impetus for sustained growth. However, difficulties in efficiently implementing infrastructure projects mean that the planned investments' potential gains may not be realised. In many respects, the region is doing well in implementing its infrastructure projects. More generally, recent actual capital expenditure has been close to budget appropriations or estimates in many countries in the region (Table 4). Nevertheless, delays in completing infrastructure projects are still common in developing countries, induced by factors such as reduced funding, communications failures, delayed disbursements, issues regarding contractors' site management, and legislative or regulatory barriers.

Table 4. **Recent capital expenditure in selected Emerging Asian countries**

Country	Time period	Budget appropriation or expected expenditure	Actual expenditure
Lao PDR	FY 2014/15	LAK 10.7 trillion	LAK 11.4 trillion
Philippines	FY 2017	PHP 773.3 billion	PHP 858.1 billion
Singapore	FY 2017	SGD 18.8 billion	SGD 17.8 billion
Thailand	FY 2017	THB 632.6 billion	THB 380.8 billion
India	2016/17	INR 3.1 trillion	INR 2.8 trillion

Note: Singapore totals refer to "development expenditure", which includes "expenses that represent a longer-term investment or result in the formation of a capitalisable asset".
Source: OECD Development Centre compilation, based on national sources.

Lastly, rising trade protectionism in some countries has the potential to soften growth in the region. While this risk is mostly beyond the control of Emerging Asian economies, the region stands to cope with the potential drags better by deepening intra- and inter-regional integration. This can be done by aligning trade standards and regulations as well as fostering trade agreements. Over the last few years, progress has been made in terms of reducing tariffs within ASEAN while free trade agreements beyond ASEAN are gaining momentum. However, the scope remains ample for co-operation in streamlining non-tariff barriers (NTMs), despite the initiatives that have been undertaken to address this issue. The use of NTMs is still prevalent among ASEAN member countries. In 2015, it was recorded that all ASEAN countries implemented all types of technical measures, which include sanitary and phytosanitary measures (SPS), technical barriers to trade (TBT) and pre-shipment inspection, and other formalities. All countries have also used non-technical measures, which include non-automatic licensing, quotas, prohibitions and quantity control measures other than for SPS or TBT, and price-control measures, including additional taxes and charges.

Chapter 2: Emerging Asia in the era of cross-border e-commerce

E-commerce is an increasingly important form of economic activity. These interactions and transactions can take place between governments, businesses and consumers. The cross-border business-to-business (B2B) and business-to-consumer (B2C) transactions in Emerging Asia look set to drastically reshape trade and business in the region. E-commerce growth in Asia has been the fastest in the world, with China leading the region. China is the world's largest B2C e-commerce market and among the frontrunners of cross-border e-commerce. Cross-border B2B e-commerce has been growing steadily since the 1990s. Growth accelerated in the 21st century with the expansion and deepening of global value chains (GVCs). While B2B still dominates cross-border e-commerce, international B2C e-commerce has been growing faster than B2B transactions.

While the e-commerce market remains smaller than traditional markets, further growth in e-commerce is expected in the future in the region and globally. From 2015 to 2021, the region's total B2C e-commerce market revenue is expected to increase from about USD 320 billion (US dollars) to more than USD 900 billion (Figure 1). Emerging Asia also accounts for a disproportionate share of Internet and e-commerce users, a trend that is expected to continue. The region accounted for 50% of the world's Internet population in 2015. Emerging Asia will host about 60% of total Internet users and a large number of e-commerce users by the end of 2021, thanks to its growing population and Internet penetration rate (Figure 2).

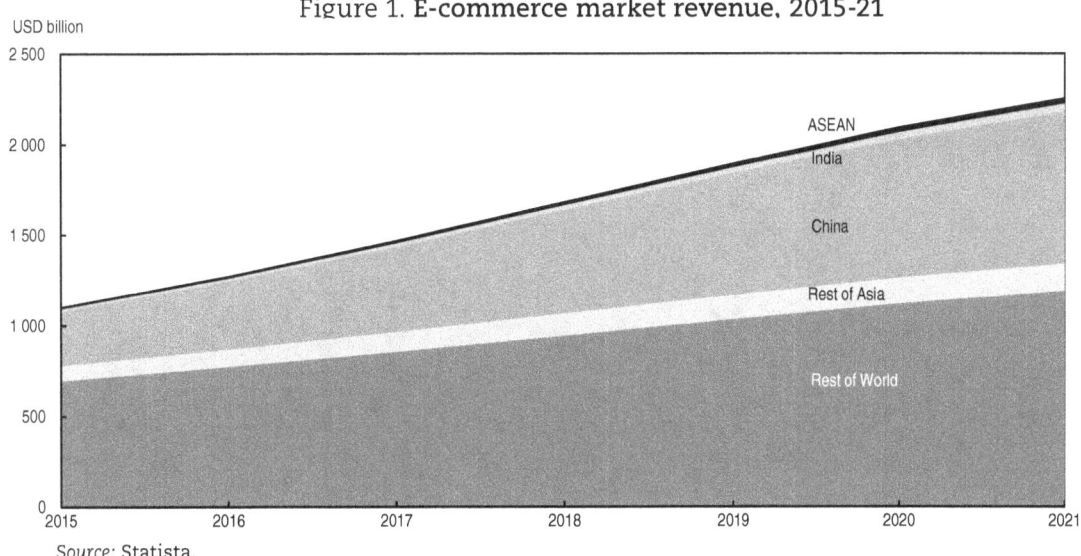

Figure 1. **E-commerce market revenue, 2015-21**

Source: Statista.
StatLink https://doi.org/10.1787/888933799587

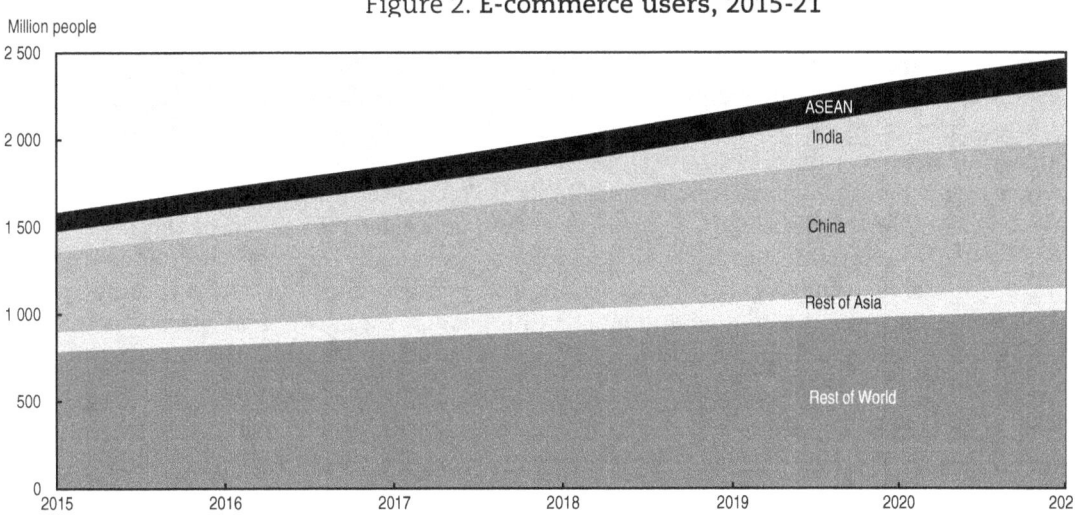

Figure 2. **E-commerce users, 2015-21**

Source: Statista.
StatLink https://doi.org/10.1787/888933799606

The scale of e-commerce in the region and the potential for its further development are the result of multiple factors, including levels of ICT use, the development of ICT infrastructure, transportation infrastructure and logistics capabilities, the use of e-payment systems, and the legal and regulatory environment.

The percentage of the population using the Internet has risen steadily across the region in recent years, although significant differences still exist between countries. In high-income countries like Singapore and Brunei Darussalam, as well as in middle-income Malaysia, the figure is higher than in other countries in the region (Figure 3). Involvement in GVCs and second mover advantages have helped firms in Emerging Asia to become relatively quick adopters of the new technologies needed to participate in cross-border e-commerce. Businesses in the region – particularly those in China, Indonesia, Malaysia and Thailand – have relatively high rates of technology use, though engagement in e-commerce also varies within countries in the region, with smaller firms less likely to take part.

Figure 3. **Internet users as a percentage of population, 2000-16**

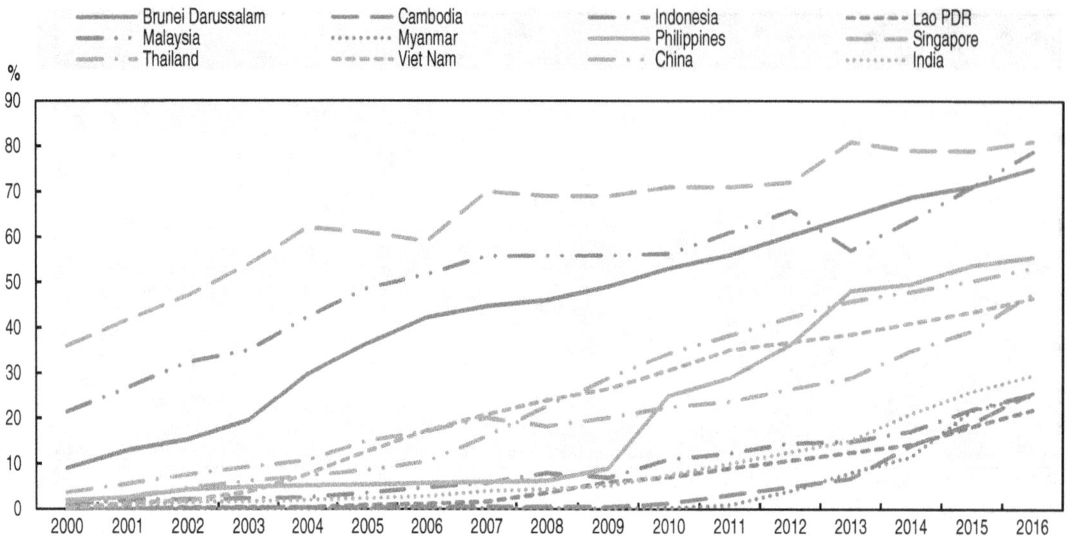

Source: World Bank (2017), *World Development Indicators*.
StatLink https://doi.org/10.1787/888933799625

The growth of e-commerce depends upon the development of extensive and high-quality Internet connections, and significant improvements are needed to ICT infrastructure in much of the region. Broadband Internet speeds, measured by the connection speeds of Internet Protocol version 4 (IPv4) addresses, are below the global average in much of the region, for example (Table 5). Geography and financing challenges have been barriers to the spread of fibre-optic connections across much of the region, though rates of mobile Internet use are high and can be especially important to residents of rural areas. Mobile technologies are also playing a large role in the growth of e-commerce in the region. However, broadband and mobile Internet accesses are expensive relative to income levels in several countries in the region, making access unaffordable for many.

In addition to ICT infrastructure, e-commerce, like traditional forms of business, still depends on transport infrastructure and logistics services for the trade and delivery of physical goods. E-commerce places higher demands on speed and transparency, posing additional challenges to storage, parcel delivery and express postal services. Since Emerging Asia faces obstacles in these areas, the development of e-commerce will require additional efforts in terms of both physical connectivity and trade-supporting services.

Table 5. **IPv4 addresses by broadband connection speed in Emerging Asia, Q1 2017**

Country	% Above 4 Mbps	% Above 10 Mbps	% Above 15 Mbps
Indonesia	76 (71)	18 (68)	5 (69)
Malaysia	72 (80)	32 (52)	14 (52)
Philippines	39 (107)	11 (78)	6.2 (63)
Singapore	94 (17)	72 (4)	51 (6)
Thailand	97 (4)	72 (5)	43 (13)
Viet Nam	86 (49)	37 (48)	11 (57)
China	81 (59)	20 (62)	5 (70)
India	42 (104)	19 (64)	10 (58)
World average	82	45	28

Note: The number in the bracket indicates the country's global ranking.
Source: Akamai (2017), *State of the Internet Connectivity Report*.

Safe and reliable e-payment systems are also important in facilitating e-commerce transactions. Cash on delivery, however, remains the preferred payment method in many Emerging Asian countries, especially those in Southeast Asia, though it is not a viable option for transactions across borders. Building and maintaining the e-payment system requires intensive resources in terms of capital, technology and people. This will be a big challenge for those Emerging Asian countries whose domestic banking and financial sectors are still at an early stage of development, though digital technologies also offer opportunities for improving financial access.

Legal and regulatory reforms are needed to facilitate fair competition and prevent the creation of grey zones of international trade associated with problems such as tax evasion, fake products and violations of intellectual property rights (IPRs). Much of the region has already enacted or drafted laws on key areas affecting e-commerce: electronic transactions, privacy, cybercrime, consumer protection, content regulation and domain names (Table 6). Taxation is another important issue, which can be complicated by cross-border e-commerce, and several countries in the region are implementing or considering new rules for taxing e-commerce. Data protection, privacy and security measures will play key roles in increasing confidence in the use of online platforms.

Table 6. **E-commerce laws in ASEAN Member States, 2013**

Country	Electronic transactions	Privacy	Cybercrime	Consumer protection	Content regulation	Domain names
Brunei Darussalam	Enacted	n.a.	Enacted	Partial	Enacted	Enacted
Cambodia	Draft	n.a.	Draft	n.a.	Draft	Enacted
Indonesia	Enacted	Partial	Enacted	Partial	Enacted	Enacted
Lao PDR	Enacted	n.a.	n.a.	Draft	Enacted	Partial
Malaysia	Enacted	Enacted	Enacted	Enacted	Enacted	Enacted
Myanmar	Enacted	n.a.	Enacted	Enacted	Enacted	Enacted
Philippines	Enacted	Enacted	Enacted	Enacted	n.a.	Enacted
Singapore	Enacted	Enacted	Enacted	Enacted	Enacted	Enacted
Thailand	Enacted	Partial	Enacted	Enacted	Partial	Partial
Viet Nam	Enacted	Partial	Enacted	Enacted	Enacted	Enacted

Source: UNCTAD (2013), *Review of E-commerce Legislation Harmonization in the Association of Southeast Asian Nations*.

The importance of developing e-commerce capabilities is widely recognised in the region; expanding e-commerce for its own sake and to support policy goals is a priority in the medium-term national development plans of several Emerging Asian countries. Achieving goals for the sector will require efforts by policy makers on improving connectivity, addressing constraints related to skills and human capital development, ensuring digital security and consumer protection, and pursuing regional and international co-operation.

While the public sector should take the lead in infrastructure development, to improve connectivity in terms of reach and quality, governments should strive for a multi-stakeholder approach to infrastructure development, broader regional co-operation and more vibrant market competition. Strengthened market competition should also help to improve logistics and Internet services and to lower prices.

Skilled workers and knowledgeable consumers will be needed to drive the ongoing development of e-commerce, which is a knowledge-intensive area of economic activity. Workers will also need to adapt to increasingly sophisticated global value chains supported by digital technologies, to get used to changing technologies and to participate in the innovation that supports competitiveness. Emerging Asia will need to leverage its considerable human resource potential to succeed in this environment. Many Emerging Asian countries lack digital literacy, and this negatively affects Internet penetration and can hold back smaller firms in particular. Improvements can be made by including digital literacy courses in educational curricula, providing sufficient equipment such as computers to schools to implement these courses, and offering other training programmes. Of the eight jurisdictions in Emerging Asia included in the OECD's 2012 Programme for International Student Assessment (PISA) survey, a majority of students had access to at least one home computer in all jurisdictions except Indonesia and Viet Nam (Figure 4).

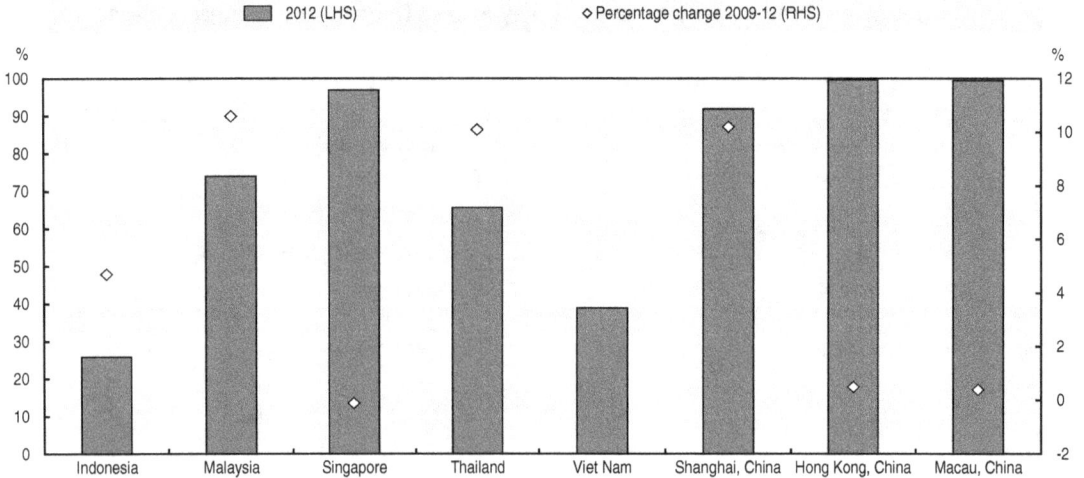

Figure 4. **Students with at least one computer at home, 2009-12**

Note: Percentage change in 2009-12 is not available for Viet Nam.
Source: OECD (2015), PISA 2012 Database, www.oecd.org/pisa/pisaproducts/pisa2012database-downloadabledata.htm.
StatLink https://doi.org/10.1787/888933799644

To improve digital security and consumer protection, countries will need to provide their consumer-protection enforcement agencies with the authority to investigate, pursue, obtain and, where appropriate, share relevant information and evidence, particularly on matters relating to cross-border fraudulent and deceptive commercial practices. Many countries in Emerging Asia still have no national legislation to support cross-border e-commerce and existing laws may not be suitable for managing disputes. Authorities should co-operate with foreign consumer-protection enforcement agencies and other appropriate foreign counterparts.

International co-operation is relevant in multiple policy areas related to e-commerce, including the harmonisation of regulatory frameworks and the establishment of rules ensuring free data flows, fair play, competition and security. Moreover, when e-commerce involves buyers and sellers in different countries, transactions are subjected to almost all issues that apply to other forms of trade, meaning that co-operation on trade facilitation would be beneficial. Regional measures – such as the ASEAN Agreement on E-commerce that ASEAN countries are currently discussing – and multilateral trade negotiations are both important areas of international co-operation on e-commerce to be pursued.

Chapter 1

Macroeconomic assessments and economic outlook for Emerging Asia

> Emerging Asian economies are projected to grow steadily in 2018 and 2019. The prognosis is backed by generally robust readings in leading consumption and investment indicators. Even though central banks have started raising their policy rates largely on concerns related to inflation and exchange rates, they have utilised other instruments in their toolkits to keep market liquidity ample. Viet Nam and Philippines will still lead the ASEAN-5 with Indonesia, Malaysia and Thailand projected to have contrasting GDP growth trends. Cambodia, Lao PDR and Myanmar are set to maintain their pace of economic expansion through 2019. Brunei Darussalam looks to build on growth momentum seen in 2017 whereas Singapore's GDP growth is estimated to marginally decline. Outside of ASEAN, China's growth will moderate in 2018 and 2019. In contrast, India, which managed to navigate obstacles tied with the lagged demonetisation effects and sales tax reform quite well, is expected to grow faster during the period. Challenges for maintaining robust growth are the rising interest rate in advanced economies amid changing domestic macroeconomic landscape, the implementation of planned infrastructure projects and the acceleration of regional integration amidst rising protectionism.

Introduction

Economic growth in Emerging Asia – Southeast Asia, China and India – remains robust: it expanded by 6.5% in 2017, slightly stronger than in 2016. Southeast Asia grew substantially faster in 2017 than in the previous year, with eight of the ten economies of the Association of Southeast Asian Nations (ASEAN) posting higher growth rates. (ASEAN groups together Brunei Darussalam, Cambodia, Indonesia, Lao PDR, Malaysia, Myanmar, the Philippines, Singapore, Thailand and Viet Nam). China's growth rate surpassed the government's target, while India managed to navigate quite well the growth obstacles tied to lagged demonetisation effects and the sales tax reform. Strong economic growth in Emerging Asia is projected to continue in 2018 and 2019 (Figure 1.1). This prognosis is backed by generally robust domestic demand. Central banks have started raising their policy rates, largely on concerns related to inflation and exchange rates, but they have used other instruments to keep market liquidity ample. External demand is likely to be relatively reserved, in light of the new tariff measures implemented by some economies. Many Emerging Asian countries are also planning to rein in government spending.

Optimism in capital markets has softened, but Emerging Asian economies' external positions have remained mostly stable so far. Current account balances have improved in a number of regional economies, while foreign direct investment (FDI) inflows show an even more encouraging picture. Inflation has picked up in some countries, and the build-up of price pressures has prompted some central banks to take a more proactive stance, although the prevailing rates are still within tolerance bands. To maintain growth, Emerging Asia must cope with the following challenges: the impact of rising interest rates in advanced economies, in particular the United States, on Emerging Asian economies; the implementation of planned infrastructure projects; and acceleration of regional integration amidst rising protectionism.

Figure 1.1. **Real GDP growth of Southeast Asia, China and India**
Comparison between 2017, 2018 and 2019 growth rates, in percentage

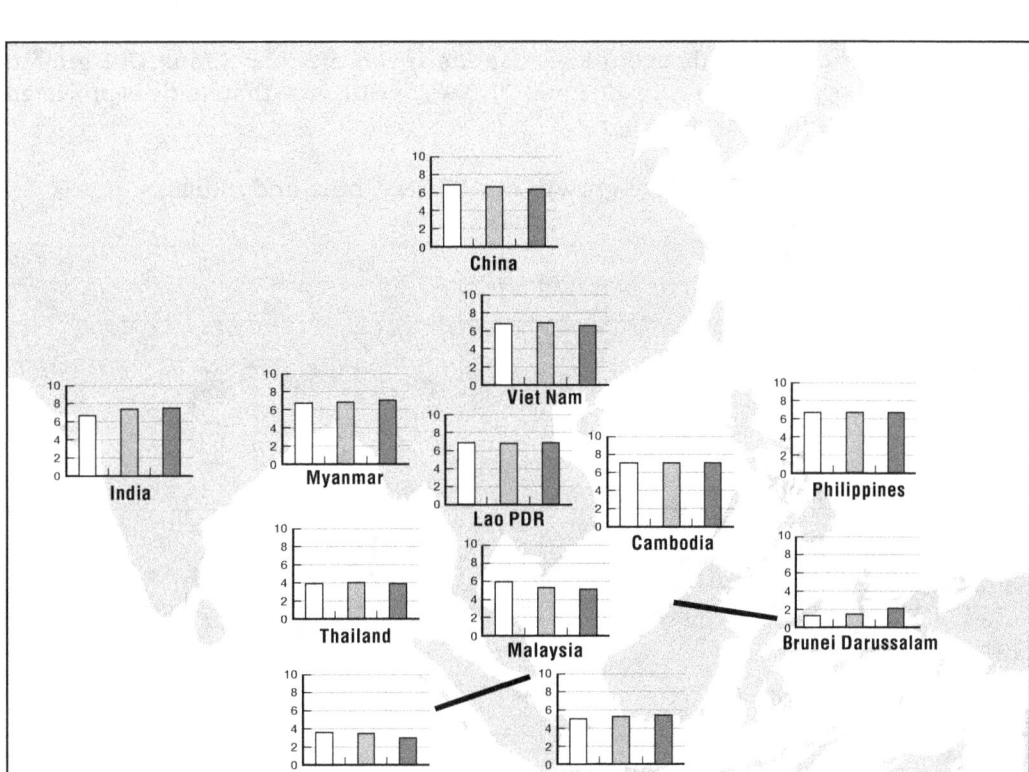

Source: OECD Development Centre, MPF-2018 (Medium-term Projection Framework).
StatLink https://doi.org/10.1787/888933799663

Overview and main findings

Emerging Asia's aggregate gross domestic product (GDP) growth is expected to firm up to 6.6% in 2018 and 6.5% in 2019 (Table 1.1). Southeast Asia's economy is estimated to grow at a steady pace of 5.3% in the next two years on the back of resilient domestic demand in many countries, though trade prospects are uncertain. In China, GDP growth is forecast to nudge downwards in 2018 and 2019 while GDP growth in India is projected to increase during the same period.

Table 1.1. **Real GDP growth in ASEAN, China and India**
Annual percentage change

	2016	2017	2018	2019
ASEAN-5 countries				
Indonesia	5.0	5.1	5.3	5.4
Malaysia	4.2	5.9	5.3	5.1
Philippines	6.9	6.7	6.7	6.7
Thailand	3.3	3.9	4.0	3.9
Viet Nam	6.2	6.8	6.9	6.6
Brunei Darussalam and Singapore				
Brunei Darussalam	-2.5	1.3	1.5	2.1
Singapore	2.4	3.6	3.5	3.0
CLM countries				
Cambodia	6.9	7.0	7.0	7.0
Lao PDR	7.0	6.9	6.8	6.9
Myanmar	5.9	6.8	6.9	7.1
China and India				
China	6.7	6.9	6.7	6.4
India	7.1	6.7	7.4	7.5
Average of ASEAN-10	4.8	5.3	5.3	5.3
Average of Emerging Asia	6.4	6.5	6.6	6.5

Notes: The cut-off date for data used is 18 June 2018. ASEAN and Emerging Asia growth rates are the weighted averages of the individual economies subsumed. Cambodia and Myanmar's 2017 data are preliminary estimates. The data of India and Myanmar follow fiscal years. For Myanmar, 2018 refers to the interim six-month period from April 2018 to September 2018, while 2019 refers to the fiscal year from October 2018 to September 2019. The projections of China, India and Indonesia are based on the OECD Economic Outlook No. 103 (database).
Source: OECD Development Centre, *Medium-term Projection Framework* (MPF-2018).

Indonesia's GDP growth will marginally improve to 5.3% in 2018 and 5.4% in 2019 on promising investment trends and robust consumer-demand indicators, anchored by wage adjustments, the hosting of the Asian Games and upcoming presidential elections. GDP growth in the first quarter (Q1) of 2018 was 5.1% more or less the same pace as observed in Q4 2017 (Table 1.2). **Malaysia**'s economic expansion is projected to moderate to 5.3% in 2018 and 5.1% in 2019 from 5.9% in 2017, largely in line with its average growth rate since 2010, though there are some uncertainties about the new administration's policies. The decision to review large infrastructure investment projects could dampen fixed investment growth. On the upside, private consumption indicators and exports are moving along relatively well. Data in Q1 2018 show that GDP growth has eased to 5.4%, from 5.6% in the same period last year. The **Philippines** is estimated to replicate its 2017 GDP growth of 6.7% in 2018 and in 2019. Government spending and public investment will likely anchor economic growth, with private consumption facing some friction and exports substantially weakening. Data in Q1 2018 show that the Philippine economy expanded by 6.8%, about 30 basis points faster than in Q1 2017. GDP growth in **Thailand** is expected to come in at 4.0% in 2018 and 3.9% in 2019. Exports are still growing strongly, benefitting the domestic industrial sector. Private consumption indicators point to an increase in expenditures, even as the government plans to continue consolidating its fiscal position. The economy started 2018 with an encouraging 4.8% expansion in Q1 2018, up from 3.4% in Q1 2017. In **Viet Nam**, GDP is projected to grow by 6.9% in 2018 and 6.6% in 2019. Data in the first half (H1) of 2018 showed a GDP growth of 7.1% (7.5% in Q1 and 6.8% in Q2), up from 5.7% in H1 2017. Private consumption is expected to remain robust. However, exports and investment intake are showing signs of moderating.

Table 1.2. **Recent real GDP growth in ASEAN, China and India**
Quarterly, year-on-year percentage change

	Q1 2017	Q2 2017	Q3 2017	Q4 2017	Q1 2018
ASEAN-5 countries					
Indonesia	5.0	5.0	5.1	5.2	5.1
Malaysia	5.6	5.8	6.2	5.9	5.4
Philippines	6.5	6.6	7.2	6.5	6.8
Thailand	3.4	3.9	4.3	4.0	4.8
Viet Nam	5.2	6.3	7.5	7.7	7.5
Brunei Darussalam and Singapore					
Brunei Darussalam	-1.3	0.2	1.3	5.2	—
Singapore	2.5	2.8	5.5	3.6	4.4
China and India					
China	6.9	6.9	6.8	6.8	6.8
India	5.6	6.3	7.0	7.7	—

Notes: The cut-off date for data used is 18 June 2018. Quarterly data are not available for Cambodia, Lao PDR and Myanmar. Data for India follow fiscal years.
Source: OECD Development Centre based on CEIC and national sources.

Brunei Darussalam's economy grew in 2017 for the first time since 2012, and it is expected to expand by 1.5% in 2018 and by 2.1% in 2019. Higher global oil prices should bode well for exports, fiscal space and the domestic labour market. In **Singapore**, the economy is expected to grow by 3.5% in 2018 and by 3.0% in 2019. Data in Q1 2018 show an economic expansion rate of 4.4%, up from 2.5% in Q1 2017, largely on the strength of exports. However, offshore shipments, which underpin a large portion of domestic industrial production and some services segments, could face stiff headwinds due to the new tariff schedules in some large economies. The realisation of planned large transportation infrastructure projects should buttress downside risks.

In **Cambodia**, GDP is expected to grow annually by 7.0% in 2018 and 2019. Construction activities will help keep domestic consumption resilient. Exports have also grown sizeably so far in 2018, although substantial risks are looming. In **Lao PDR**, GDP growth is estimated to settle at 6.8% in 2018 and to rise to 6.9% in 2019. The expansion of overseas electricity deals and the strong influx of foreign direct investment are a boon to the country's growth prospects in the near term. In **Myanmar**, the economy is expected to grow by about 6.9% in the interim six-month period from April 2018 to September 2018 (given the change in fiscal year coverage) and by 7.1% in fiscal year 2019 (October 2018 to September 2019). Consumption will likely remain buoyant, on wage adjustments. The economy should also benefit from infrastructure projects that have been pushed forward to clear the pipeline during the interim period.

China's GDP growth is projected to moderate to 6.7% in 2018 and to 6.4% in 2019. Household consumption is expected to maintain a relatively steady expansion rate on the back of robust real disposable income growth. A potential source of downside risk is escalating trade tensions, leading to tariffs on an increasing number of goods. This could hurt exports and potentially spill over to investment by export-oriented firms. Recent data show that China's GDP grew by 6.8% in Q1 2018, marginally lower than the 6.9% in Q1 2017. Meanwhile, **India**'s economic growth is poised to rise to 7.4% in 2018 and 7.5% in 2019. Private spending should benefit from rising credit growth. Improvements in revenue intake should also help the government expand spending coverage. The issues related to banks' non-performing assets will require careful attention.

Other key points of the economic outlook and assessment

- Overall, the external positions of Emerging Asian economies have remained stable so far. Current account balances have improved in a number of economies in the region. FDI data show an even more encouraging picture. Overall risk perception in the region, as suggested by the credit default swap spreads, has risen since mid-January 2018, although the spreads indicate that the degree of concern is still relatively limited.

- Monetary authorities in Emerging Asia have started raising policy rates, mainly on the grounds of rising inflation and weakening of some local currencies. However, they have also used the mandated reserve requirement ratio for banks to keep the system liquid, presumably to isolate the direct monetary policy impact on exchange rates, inflation and domestic credit flows. Headline inflation in several Emerging Asian countries has been climbing since the end of 2017, propelled partly by the rise in global oil prices and the strengthening of the US dollar. Local currencies like the Philippine peso, Indonesian rupiah and Indian rupee have depreciated this year.

- Overall, the fiscal positions of Emerging Asian economies are relatively sound. The fiscal policy direction, however, is mixed. Revenue performances (i.e. revenue-to-GDP) diverged across the region from 2016 to 2017. While the revenue ratios of Cambodia, the Philippines, Singapore and Viet Nam have either improved or remained stable, the ratios of Brunei Darussalam, China, India, Indonesia, Lao PDR, Malaysia and Thailand have deteriorated.

- Economies in the region will need to cope with several challenges to maintain robust growth. Firstly, the impact of rising interest rates in advanced economies, in particular the United States, on Emerging Asia requires vigilant attention. The potential that this could trigger substantial capital outflows cannot be set aside considering the recent broadening of domestic inflation pressures, weakening of currencies in the region, and growing credit risk perception. With domestic interest rates rising more sternly, consumption and investment prospects could be diminished, which will consequently negatively influence trade.

- Secondly, the extent of the effectiveness of infrastructure project implementation can be both an upside and a downside risk to economic activity. Timely and efficient implementation of infrastructure plans can be a strong impetus for sustained growth. However, long delays and other challenges can result in higher financing cost to public and private institutions involved as well as economic opportunity costs.

- Lastly, rising trade protectionism in major economies can soften growth in the region. While this risk is mostly beyond the control of Emerging Asian economies, the region stands to cope with the potential drags better by deepening intra- and inter-regional integration by aligning trade standards and regulations as well as fostering trade agreements.

Recent macroeconomic developments and near-term prospects

ASEAN-5 (Indonesia, Malaysia, the Philippines, Thailand and Viet Nam)

Indonesia

Indonesia's economy grew by 5.1% in 2017, below the 5.2% target but marginally faster than the 5.0% expansion rate in 2016.[1] Private consumption growth remained steady at 5.0%, supported by declining unemployment rate and faster growth in commercial and rural bank loans to individuals (Figure 1.2). Nominal FDI inflows, which quadrupled in 2017 after a steep 77.0% fall in 2016, provided impetus to fixed capital formation. Gross export growth increased in 2017, following a two-year contraction. In particular, overseas shipments of oil and gas, agriculture, manufacturing and services saw large increases in nominal receipts in 2017. On the supply side, agricultural output expanded faster in 2017 than in 2016, benefiting from more favourable weather conditions. Manufacturing and wholesale and retail trade (WRT) also posted encouraging growth rates, largely due to stronger overseas demand and stable domestic consumption. By comparison, mining and quarrying growth narrowed slightly during the year. Financial services growth, though robust, also declined.

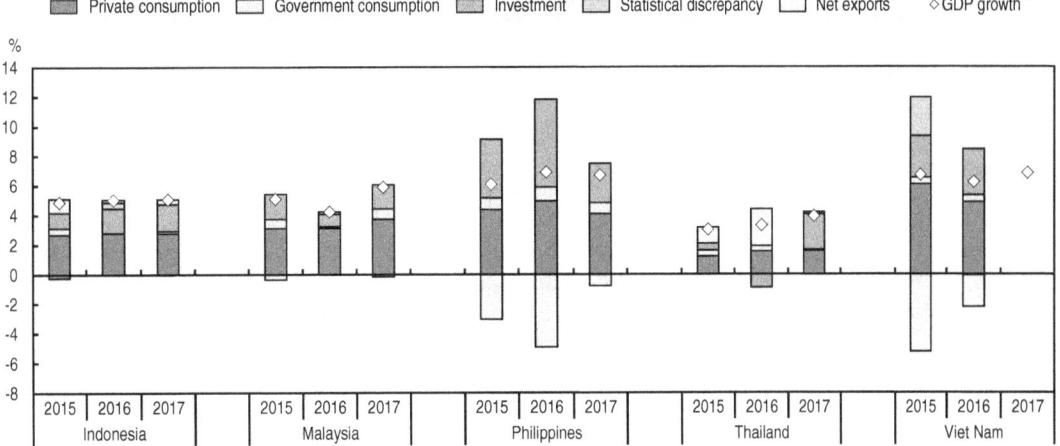

Figure 1.2. **Contribution to real GDP growth in ASEAN-5 countries, 2015-17**
Percentage points

Notes: Thailand uses chain volume measures. The sum of contributions to growth is not necessarily equal to GDP growth. Viet Nam has not yet published the demand-side components of GDP in 2017.
Source: OECD Development Centre calculations based on CEIC data.
StatLink https://doi.org/10.1787/888933799682

Indonesia's GDP growth is projected to rise to 5.3% in 2018 and to 5.4% in 2019. Private consumption will likely continue to boost growth in the coming quarters, with consumer confidence remaining upbeat (Figure 1.3). The increase in average minimum wage growth in 2018 from 2017 will favour household spending. In addition, the Asian Games in August 2018 will be a one-off boost, as will the run-off to presidential elections in April 2019. However, the central bank's 1 percentage point rate hike in May-June 2018 could potentially be an offsetting factor. Fixed investment is on track to maintain its expansion rate, based on the momentum of capital imports and FDI. The 15th and 16th economic policy packages have encouraged investment with their focus on improving logistics and hastening investment-related procedures. Nonetheless, government spending growth is set to remain tempered this year. The nominal growth of goods exports receipts from January to April 2018 has also weakened; this slowdown includes oil and gas exports, despite the rise in global energy prices. In the first three months of 2018, Indonesia's GDP grew by 5.1%, marginally faster than the 5.0% rate in Q1 2017. Fixed investment growth increased during the period. Export growth decreased slightly but remained brisk at 6.2%, while private consumption and government spending growth held steady at 5.0% and 2.7%, respectively.

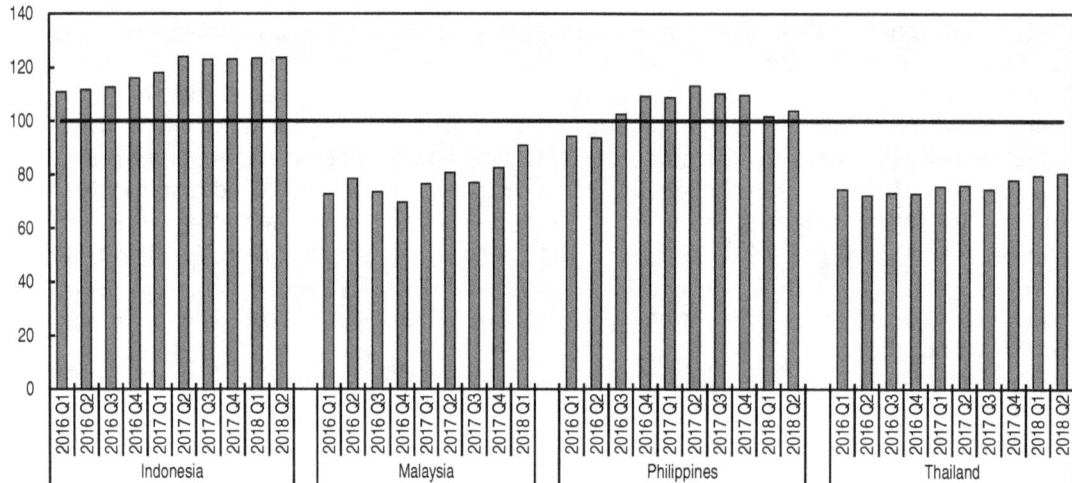

Figure 1.3. **Consumer confidence indices in selected ASEAN countries, 2016-18**

Note: All indices are adjusted to set 100 as neutral confidence point. Data of Indonesia and Thailand are as of May 2018.
Source: OECD Development Centre calculations based on CEIC and national sources.
StatLink https://doi.org/10.1787/888933799701

Malaysia

Malaysia's GDP growth improved to 5.9% in 2017, up from 4.2% in 2016, fuelled by broad-based demand-side pickup. Private consumption grew by 7.0% in 2017, from 6.0% in 2016, which can be attributed to the stable labour market, robust bank lending and the expansion of the government's targeted subsidies. The unemployment rate remained low in 2017. Nominal bank loan disbursement to households rose modestly in 2017, after contracting in 2016. Moreover, allotments under the monetary aid programme for low-income groups (e.g. Bantuan Rakyat 1Malaysia) were raised, while the lifestyle tax relief was expanded. The surge in government spending growth from 0.9% in 2016 to 5.4% in 2017 is another bright spot, prompted in part by the central government's improved budgetary revenues in 2017. Fixed investments growth more than doubled, from 2.7% in 2016 to 6.2% in 2017; private outlays largely accounted for this growth, despite the decline in the nominal value of FDI inflows during the year. Finally, gross exports increased by 9.6% in 2017, the fastest pace since 2010, led by crude materials, mineral fuels, machineries and manufactures. On the supply side, agriculture rebounded strongly, growing by 7.2% in 2017 after contracting by 5.2% in 2016, on the bumper harvest of crops like rice and wheat resulting from a good monsoon. Manufacturing, WRT and financial services also posted stronger growth, feeding off strong domestic and offshore demand.

Malaysia's economic growth is projected to slow down to 5.3% in 2018 and to 5.1% in 2019. Manufacturing nominal sales growth rose 8.2% in April from 6.5% in Q1 2018, but, slower than the 15.6% in April 2017. Distributive trade sales nominal growth follows a similar trend. Nominal goods export receipts growth expressed in US dollars is still rising (Figure 1.4). However, in terms of Malaysian ringgit, growth has been slowing due to local currency appreciation since the beginning of 2017. On the upside, despite the central bank's rate tightening, loan disbursements to households increased by 14.6% from

January to April 2018, up from 2.2% in the same period in 2017, largely due to real estate, personal and credit card purchases. Consumer pessimism has ebbed, based on April 2018 data, compared with the same period a year ago. In addition, average pay per worker (in real prices) has grown faster in manufacturing sector, based on data through April 2018. The increase in approved manufacturing capital investment and FDI inflows in Q1 2018 is encouraging for fixed investments in the coming quarters; however, the data does not yet reflect the decision of Malaysia's new government to review some of the infrastructure projects. In addition to the infrastructure projects, the new government also plans to implement structural and administrative changes that could affect the economic growth path (Box 1.1). GDP growth in Q1 2018 eased to 5.4%, from 5.6% in the same period in 2017. Private consumption largely lifted the economy, as the growth of fixed investment, government spending and exports all decelerated substantially.

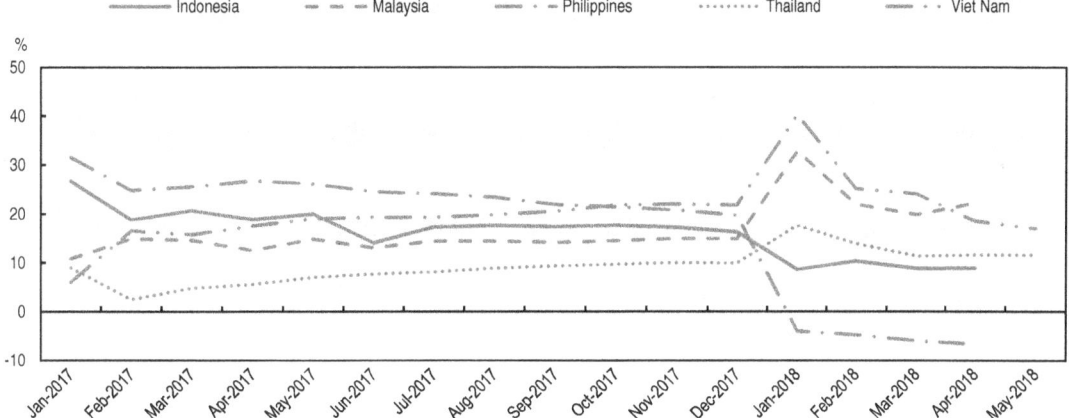

Figure 1.4. **Value of goods exports from ASEAN-5 countries, 2017-18**
YOY YTD growth

Note: Calculations are based on levels data in US dollars.
Source: OECD Development Centre calculations based on CEIC data.
StatLink https://doi.org/10.1787/888933799720

Box 1.1. **Malaysia is undergoing restructuring with the new Pakatan Harapan government**

Malaysia's 14th general election, held on 9 May 2018, saw a victory for the opposition Alliance of Hope (Pakatan Harapan), which unseated the incumbent National Front (Barisan Nasional) government. The Alliance of Hope won 113 of the 222 total seats in Parliament, compared with 79 seats for the National Front coalition. This is a milestone in Malaysia's history: the same coalition has governed the country since its independence from the British in 1957. Dr Mahathir Mohamad, who had retired as Prime Minister in 2003, was appointed the seventh Prime Minister of Malaysia at the age of 92, unseating his former protégé and National Front leader, Najib Razak.

Although the new government has been in power only a few months and its policy direction remains uncertain, significant fiscal, institutional and administrative changes have been made as part of the commitment highlighted by the Alliance of Hope manifesto. To achieve one of the manifesto's goals, the Malaysian government, through the Ministry of Finance, announced that the Goods and Services Tax (GST) would be reduced to zero from 1 June 2018; the tax had been set at 6% since its introduction on 1 April 2015. The new measure fulfilled the government's campaign promise to abolish the GST within its first

Box 1.1. **Malaysia is undergoing restructuring with the new Pakatan Harapan government** (cont.)

100 days in office, in an effort to reduce Malaysians' rising cost of living. However, the reduction of the GST is expected to reduce tax revenue by an estimated MYR 18 billion (Malaysian ringgits), or about 7.5% of total government revenue. Other fiscal measures are expected to be introduced to narrow the loss of revenue from GST collection and to support the reinstated petrol and diesel subsidy. The re-introduction of the Sales and Services Tax (SST) will be effective from 1 September 2018, giving consumers and businesses a three-month tax break. As of July 2018, however, the GST framework remains; this means businesses must adhere to existing rules and procedures, such as tax invoices and regular tax statement submissions, as well as the input tax-credit completion.

The Ministry of Domestic Trade, Consumerism and Cooperatives announced in May that petrol and diesel subsidies would be reinstated so that fuel prices can remain unchanged or static. Diesel and RON 95 petrol would stay at their current price, while the price of RON 97 would be revised every Wednesday. The measure is in line with the new government's commitment to stabilise retail fuel prices to reduce living costs in the country.

On national debt issues, the Ministry of Finance on 24 May 2018 confirmed that federal government debt and liabilities accounted for 80.3% of GDP as of December 2017, much higher than the 50.8% of GDP (or MYR 686.6 billion) reported by the previous government. The government's liabilities as of December 2017 comprised three parts: i) the federal government debt of MYR 686.8 billion (50.8% of GDP); ii) government guarantees of MYR 199.1 billion, or 14.6% of GDP (the government is committed to paying the debt of entities unable to make their own payment, including MYR 42.2 billion for Danainfra Nasional Bhd, MYR 26.6 billion for Prasarana Malaysia Bhd and MYR 38 billion for 1Malaysia Development Bhd [1MDB]); iii) lease payments of MYR 201.4 billion (14.9% of GDP) for public-private projects. The government must pay for rental, maintenance and other costs on a number of projects, such as the construction of schools, hospitals and roads.

Ongoing structural and administrative reforms include a 10% salary cut for ministers and the elimination of several non-essential and political government agencies. In May 2018, the Prime Minister announced that the Land Public Transport Commission, which led negotiations with Singapore for the high-speed rail project under the previous government, will be shut down; its tasks and responsibilities will be taken over by the Transport Ministry. Other agencies will be abolished, as well, including the Special Affairs Department (Jasa), the National Council of Professors, the Federal Village Development and Security Committee, Residents' Representatives Committee and the Malaysian External Intelligence Organisation. The government introduced an Economic Affairs Ministry to promote economic growth, transparency and structural reforms. The new ministry will oversee matters related to economic policy as well as the Economic Planning Unit, formerly under the supervision of the Prime Minister's Office. The Public-Private Partnership Unit, SME and Micro Credit Development Unit and selected SOEs like PETRONAS will also be placed under the jurisdiction of the new ministry.

The Philippines

The Philippines' GDP grew by 6.7% in 2017, the seventh time in the past eight years that the rate exceeded 6.0% (the exception was in 2011). Gross exports led the GDP growth push, rising by 19.5% in 2017, from 11.5% in 2016; offshore sales of electronics, mineral products and machineries made big gains last year. Private and government consumption slowed down, due in part to base effects as national elections were held in 2016. The relatively slow rollout of big-ticket projects lowered fixed investment growth in 2017. On the supply side, agriculture reversed the 1.2% contraction in 2016 and grew by 4.0% in 2017, aided by favourable weather and the surge in external demand. Manufacturing also grew at a faster rate in 2017, on strong export sales. WRT and financial services maintained the impressive growth rates of 2016, with WRT growing by 7.3%, and financial services by 7.6%.

The Philippine economy is projected to grow by 6.7% in 2018, which the country will maintain in 2019. Data at the end of Q1 2018 show an economic expansion of 6.8%, about 30 basis points faster than the same period the previous year. The increase in GDP growth was propelled mainly by government spending, which rose by 13.6%, from 0.1% a year earlier. By comparison, growth in private spending, fixed investment and gross exports weakened during the period. A similar pattern seems likely in the coming quarters. Government consumption is expected to remain buoyant; revenue intake is on track to surpass targets, as seen in the first four months of 2018. Investment has some room to grow faster than before, but this will depend on the efficiency of project rollout. Private spending can benefit from lower income-tax payments covering most workers. Some degree of monetary accommodation (exemplified by reserve requirement ratio adjustments) will help. Yet, the moderation in overseas remittances could drag down household spending growth; year-to-date year-on-year (YTD YOY) growth in remittances slid to 3.5% through April 2018, from 4.2% in the same period the previous year. Rising domestic prices, lower consumer optimism in Q1-Q2 2018 and uncertainties in tourism prospects – due to the government's decision to close a top destination for rehabilitation – can also further stifle private spending. Separately, offshore goods shipments nominal growth slowed down in the first four months of 2018; this slowdown sends a pessimistic signal to domestic production. However, the encouraging growth of the industrial production index (IPI) and net sales index in the same period suggests that the volume of orders for future shipments is somewhat picking up.

Thailand

Thailand's economy grew by 3.9% in 2017, the fastest pace since 2012, on the strength of household consumption and overseas demand. Private consumption growth rose from 3.0% in 2016 to 3.2% in 2017, helped by the moderate acceleration in household credit and the 8.8% increase in tourist arrivals (about the same rate as in 2016). Gross exports increased by 5.5%, about twice the 2.8% growth rate the previous year, led by agricultural and mineral products. Notably, fixed investment growth slowed from 2.8% in 2016 to 0.9% in 2017, reflecting the decline in construction activities. Government spending barely increased, going up by 0.5% in 2017 from 2.2% in 2016, on efforts to rein in the widening budget deficit as revenue inflows weakened during the fiscal year that ended in September 2017.

Thailand's economy is projected to grow by 4.0% in 2018 and by about 3.9% in 2019. The economy started off the year with an encouraging 4.8% expansion in Q1 2018 (up from 3.4% in Q1 2017), fuelled by a concerted increase in the growth of major demand-side components. Leading indicators suggest that economic growth is holding up well. Offshore demand remains strong, with nominal goods exports value rising by 11.9% in April-May 2018, from 10.4% in the same period a year earlier. This is mirrored by the robust IPI reading maintained from January to April 2018 (Figure 1.5). Consumer pessimism continued to recede in April 2018, from 12 months earlier. Tourist arrival growth accelerated to 14% in January-April 2018, from 3.3% in the same period a year earlier (Figure 1.6). On the other hand, growth frictions could arise from continued fiscal consolidation and uncertainties surrounding the timeframes of infrastructure projects mostly linked to the Eastern Economic Corridor (EEC) initiative. Bad loans besetting some sectors can also create difficulties as interest rates rise. The commercial bank non-performing loan (NPL) ratio of the mining and quarrying sector remains at close to 14%, while that of construction and wholesale and retail trade are both over 5.5%, although the picture has generally improved from December 2017 to March 2018.

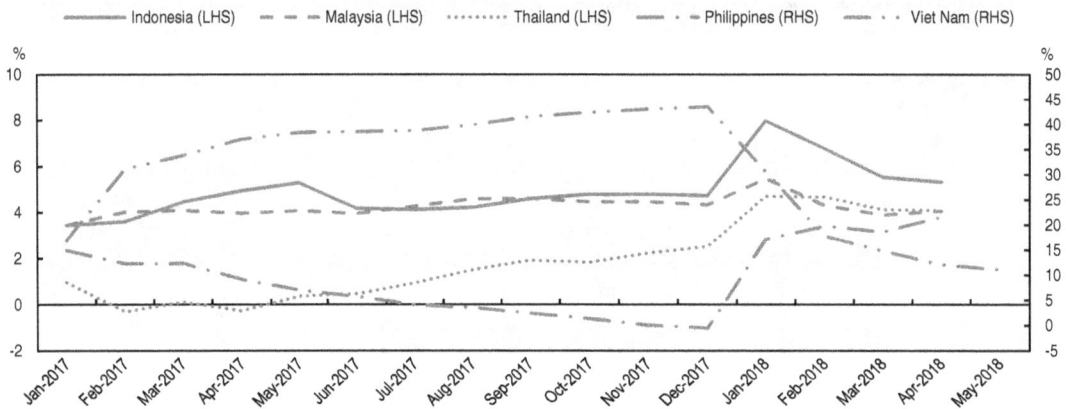

Figure 1.5. **Industrial Production Indices in ASEAN-5 countries, 2017-18**
YOY YTD growth

Note: RHS means right-hand scale, and LHS means left-hand scale.
Source: OECD Development Centre calculations based on CEIC data.
StatLink https://doi.org/10.1787/888933799739

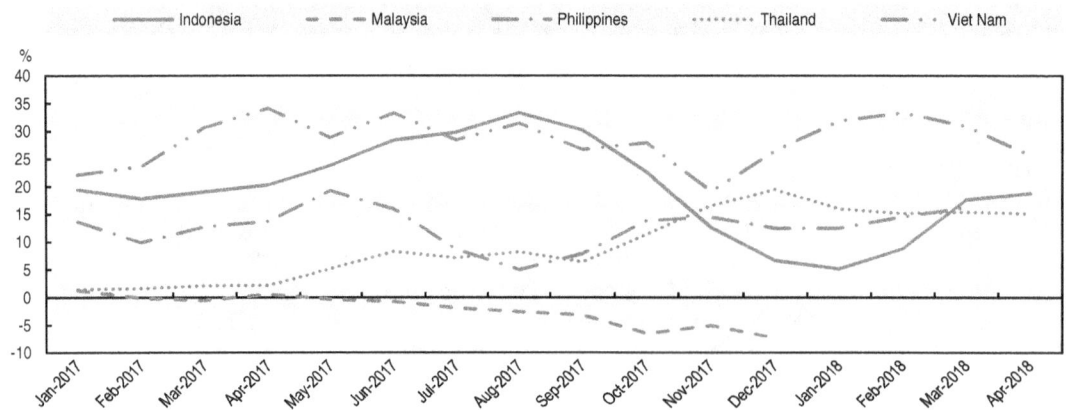

Figure 1.6. **Tourist arrivals in ASEAN-5 countries, 2017-18**
YOY growth, 3-month rolling sum

Source: OECD Development Centre calculations based on CEIC data.
StatLink https://doi.org/10.1787/888933799758

Viet Nam

Viet Nam's GDP increased by 6.8% in 2017, up from 6.2% in 2016, towed by a strong second-half performance which made up for a relatively meek first half. Export growth strongly supported economic expansion: nominal gross exports value increased by 20.3% in 2017, from 9.0% in 2016, based on balance of payments data. Shipments of phones and phone parts, electronic goods and computers (excluding phones), textiles, machinery and agricultural products all increased sizeably. Final consumption maintained a high growth rate of 7.4%, roughly unchanged from the previous year, anchored by the steady decline in the unemployment rate and the gradual but persistent rise in real earnings. State budget spending also supported economic growth, despite fiscal tightness; state budget spending (excluding interest payments) grew by 13.1% in 2017, up from 8.4% in the previous year (in nominal prices). On the supply side, manufacturing and the large services sub-sectors – WRT, accommodation and finance – have been key to propelling growth.

Viet Nam's economy is projected to grow by 6.9% in 2018 to lead the ASEAN-5 economies and by 6.6% in 2019. Data in H1 2018 – which showed a year-on-year (YOY) growth of 7.1%, (i.e. 7.5% in Q1 and 6.8% in Q2) up from 5.7% in H1 2017 – support this prognosis. Acceleration in goods exports growth underpinned this economic expansion: exports grew by 15.8% in H1 2018, though less than the 19.3% in H1 2017 (in nominal prices). The nominal value of total realised social investment capital, which grew by about 10.1% in the first six months of the year, also boosted the economy. Private sector spending, partly aided by the sharp rise in tourist arrivals, was just as robust, as suggested by the approximately 10.7% nominal growth in retail sales of consumer goods and services in the same period. Lower readings in manufacturing Purchasing Managers' Index (PMI) between February 2018 and April 2018 from a year ago, though still expanding, are in line with the softening export growth trend albeit the uptick in May 2018 suggests that offshore orders may have gained momentum anew. Additionally, total newly registered and additional capital from January to June 2018 dropped YOY by 4.4%, of which FDI registered capital decreased by about 0.3%.

Brunei Darussalam and Singapore

Brunei Darussalam

Brunei Darussalam's GDP grew by 5.2% in Q4 2017 (the fastest growth rate since Q2 2010) to lift the annual expansion rate to 1.3%, the first time it turned positive since 2012. Private consumption rose 4.1% in 2017 following a 1.3% contraction in 2016, spurred by oil price recovery and better economic prospects overall (Figure 1.7). Despite the downward adjustment to budgetary spending, the government's final consumption expenditure rose by 7.4%, from -6.5% the previous year. Fixed investment growth recovered to 8.1%, from -11.2% the previous year, thanks to enduring construction expansion. By contrast, the volume of exports dropped by 2.7% in 2017, sharper than the 1.9% decline in 2016, although higher global prices lifted the nominal revenues from shipments of crude oil, natural gas and total manufacturing goods (including miscellaneous manufactures).

Figure 1.7. **Contribution to real GDP growth in Brunei Darussalam and Singapore, 2015-17**

Percentage points

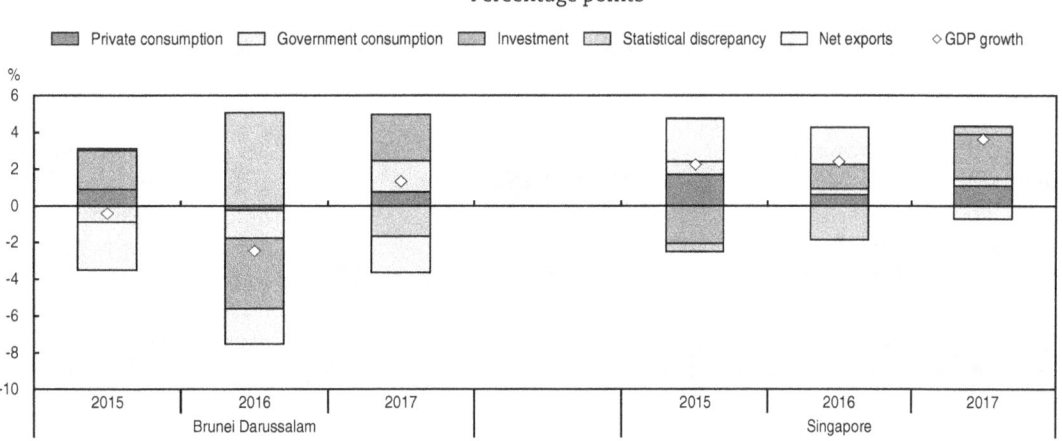

Source: OECD Development Centre calculations based on CEIC data.
StatLink https://doi.org/10.1787/888933799777

Brunei Darussalam's GDP growth is projected to rise to 1.5% in 2018 and to 2.1% in 2019. The economy stands to gain from rising oil and gas prices, which should expand the government's fiscal space. This economic growth also bodes well for labour market conditions in terms of raising wages and arresting the rise in the unemployment rate (although the rate remains benign). The generally declining trend of NPL ratio since December 2016, should help spur bank credit disbursements in the coming quarters. The year-on-year growth of outstanding commercial bank loans has contracted every quarter from September 2016 to March 2018; this contraction, largely due to asset quality concerns and economic difficulties, has eased in recent months. Moreover, construction activities are expected to continue to grow robustly in 2018.

Singapore

Singapore's GDP growth rose for the second straight year, reaching 3.6% in 2017, up from 2.4% in 2016. Gross exports – which grew by 4.1%, up from 1.1% in 2016 – provided much of the boost. Private consumption accelerated, growing from 1.7% in 2016 to 3.1% in 2017. Government spending also rose, from 3.5% in 2016 to 4.1% in 2017, although the budget balance still ended in surplus during the fiscal year. By contrast, fixed investments declined by 1.8%, largely due to a steep drop in construction spending. However, the sixfold rise in the capital inventory accumulation indicated an improving durable investment outlook. On the supply side, manufacturing surged by 10.1%, outpacing the 3.7% growth in 2016. WRT and financial services also posted faster growth rates in 2017.

Figure 1.8. **Value of goods exports from Brunei Darussalam and Singapore, 2017-18**
YOY YTD growth

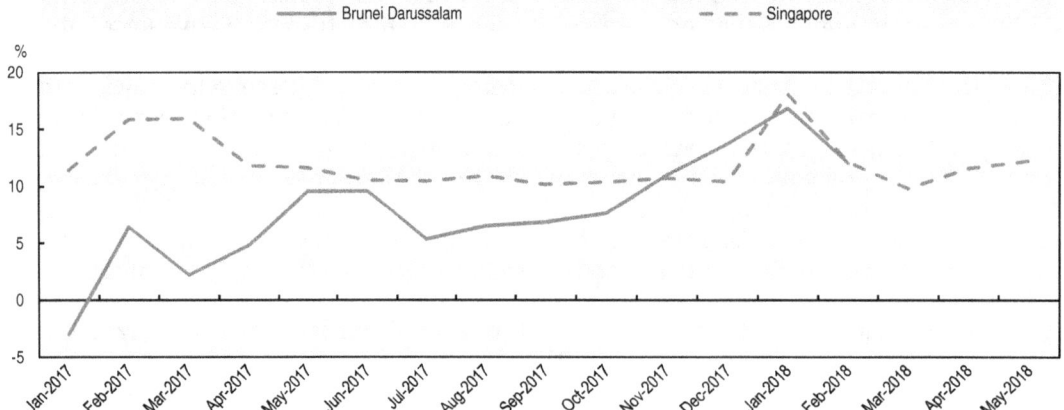

Note: Calculations are based on levels data in US dollars.
Source: OECD Development Centre calculations based on CEIC data.
StatLink https://doi.org/10.1787/888933799796

Singapore's economy is projected to grow by 3.5% in 2018 and 3.0% in 2019. GDP growth in Q1 2018 rose to 4.4%, from 2.5% in Q1 2017. Export-driven manufacturing output grew by 9.8%, slightly faster than the 8.5% growth in the previous year. The rising manufacturing PMI through June 2018 suggests that orders for future delivery continue to gain traction. Nominal goods exports value expressed in US dollars grew by 15.8% in April-May 2018, from 10% in Q1 2018 and 5.9% in April-May 2017 (Figure 1.8). Growth in the services sector (including ownership of dwellings) jumped to 4.0% from 1.7%, on the strength of activities in the financial and WRT sub-sectors. The production of construction materials, on the other hand, decreased for the seventh quarter in a row, with real estate developments remaining downbeat. New private home sales (excluding executive condominiums) rose by 38.0% in 2017, but decreased by more than 50.0% year-on-year in January-April 2018.

The planned hike in government disbursements on large rail projects should buttress the economy against possible external growth headwinds. The sustained increase in median wages and the government's decision to co-fund wage adjustments of some firms through 2020 should also help maintain private consumption growth, at least in the short run.

CLM countries (Cambodia, Lao PDR and Myanmar)

Cambodia

Cambodia's GDP grew by an estimated 7.0% in 2017, up slightly from 6.9% in 2016. The growth in the nominal value of goods exports – which rose to 27.2% in 2017, from 9.9% the previous year – played a key role in maintaining the expansion of domestic production. Offshore sales of footwear, garments, textile and rubber increased sizeably during the year. Private consumption growth remained strong, as shown by the persistent growth above 30.0% in personal loans, the 11.8% rise in tourist arrivals in 2017 (more than double the 5.0% rise in 2016) and the sharp rise in the imports of durable consumer goods such as vehicles, motorbikes and clothing. The 24.4% increase in FDI inflows (based on data as of Q3 2017), outpacing robust inflow rate of 20.8% in the same period in 2016, also boosted the economy. Interestingly, however, the value of petroleum product imports decreased by more than 35.0%.

Figure 1.9. **Contribution to real GDP growth in Cambodia, Lao PDR and Myanmar, 2015-17**

Percentage points

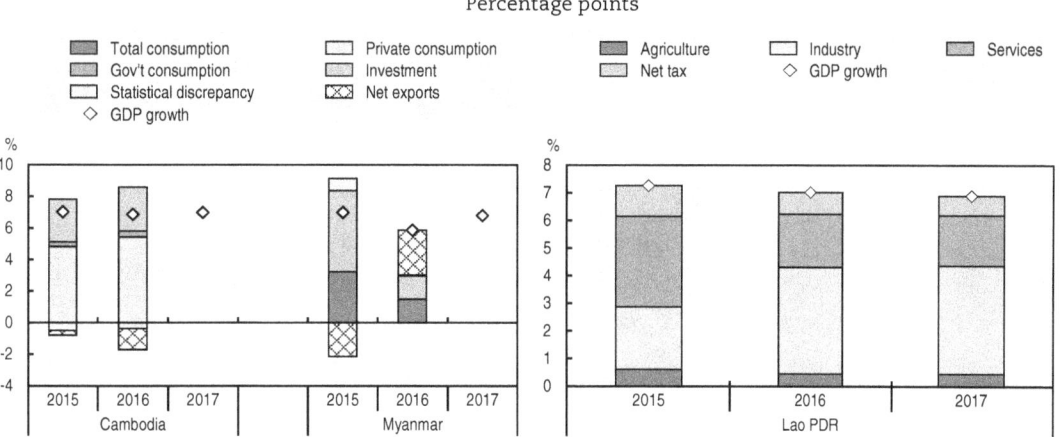

Notes: Myanmar follows the fiscal year, i.e. 2017 pertains to FY 2017-18 (April 2017-March 2018). The 2017 data of Cambodia and Myanmar are estimates. Lao PDR does not publish demand-side data. Total consumption = private consumption+government spending. Net tax = taxes minus subsidies.
Source: OECD Development Centre calculations based on CEIC data.
StatLink https://doi.org/10.1787/888933799815

In 2018 and 2019, Cambodia is expected to post a GDP growth rate of 7.0%. Nominal goods exports grew dramatically in January/February 2018, compared with the same period the previous year. Approvals of fixed-asset investments more than doubled, to USD 5.2 billion in 2017, from USD 2.4 billion in 2016. The marked rise in imports of construction materials, cement and steel in recent months suggest an increase in construction activities. Meanwhile, the opening of several malls in Phnom Penh will facilitate WRT services as well as private consumption. The general elections scheduled in July 2018 will likely result in temporary increases in government spending. In addition, the involvement of Cambodia in multilateral infrastructure projects such as those under the Greater Mekong Subregion (GMS) and Belt and Road (B&R) initiative offers an opportunity to improve existing public capital stock and reduce the cost of doing business in the country.

Lao PDR

Lao PDR's GDP grew by 6.9% in 2017, slightly below the 7.0% in 2016. Goods export receipts in nominal prices grew by a brisk 22.6% during the year, more than matching the strong 21.1% growth in 2016. Electricity exports transaction value surged by 18.3%, after doubling the previous year. Sales of agricultural products overseas (e.g. tea, spices and cereals), wood products and prepared foodstuff also rose healthily. Separately, FDI inflows growth rose to 70% in 2017, from 17.1% in 2016, mostly going to electricity generation, agriculture and mining industries. Government budgetary spending jumped by about 9.4% in 2017, reversing the contraction in 2016.

Lao PDR's GDP growth is expected to settle at 6.8% in 2018 and 6.9% in 2019, with offshore shipments, particularly power, likely to continue growing strongly (Figure 1.10). In previous years, Lao PDR exported electricity mainly to Thailand. Recently, however, the country entered into an agreement with Malaysia, signed a memorandum of understanding with Viet Nam and targets deals with Myanmar and Singapore under the Lao PDR-Thailand-Malaysia-Singapore Power Integration Project. Investment in the mineral and energy sectors is expected to grow robustly, considering the generally positive business response to regulation liberalisation so far (Box 1.2). The infrastructure spending should also be supportive of the growth so long as they do not weigh down on fiscal stability. Notably, imports of machineries and other mechanical equipment increased substantially last year. One potential offsetting factor is public budgetary spending, which will probably slacken marginally this year as the government tries to rein in spending. Strengthening the banking sector's solvency and liquidity positions appear to be the prominent challenges. Public and public guaranteed debt, which has breached 61% of GDP in 2017 based on IMF (2018a) estimates from 56.3% in 2013, is another concern.

Figure 1.10. **Value of goods exports from Cambodia, Lao PDR and Myanmar, 2016-18**

YOY YTD growth

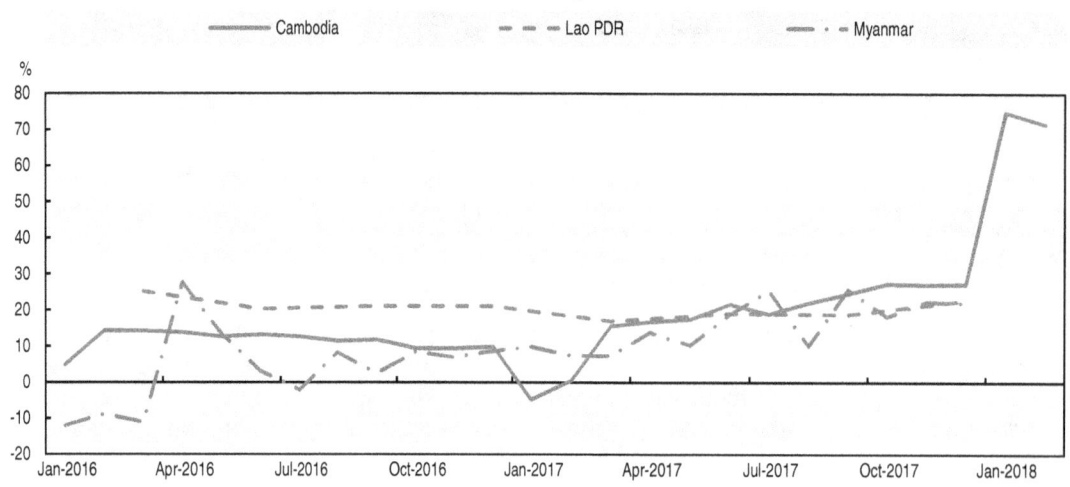

Notes: The frequency of data of Lao PDR is quarterly. Latest data of Cambodia are as of February 2018 while that of Lao PDR and Myanmar are as of December 2017. Myanmar data follow fiscal year. Calculations are based on levels data in US dollars.
Source: OECD Development Centre calculations based on CEIC data.
StatLink https://doi.org/10.1787/888933799834

Box 1.2. **Policies supporting foreign direct investment in Cambodia, Lao PDR and Myanmar**

The CLM countries (Cambodia, Lao PDR and Myanmar) have shown strong economic growth in the past years, boasting growth rates of about 7% after the global financial crisis. Robust foreign direct investment (FDI) has contributed significantly to their rapid economic expansion. The CLM countries' supportive investment policies play a big role in fostering a pro-business environment and attracting FDI from around the world (Figure 1.11). These policies include adopting investment-supporting laws and regulations, establishing special economic zones (SEZs), and forming regional and bilateral investment-promotion agreements.

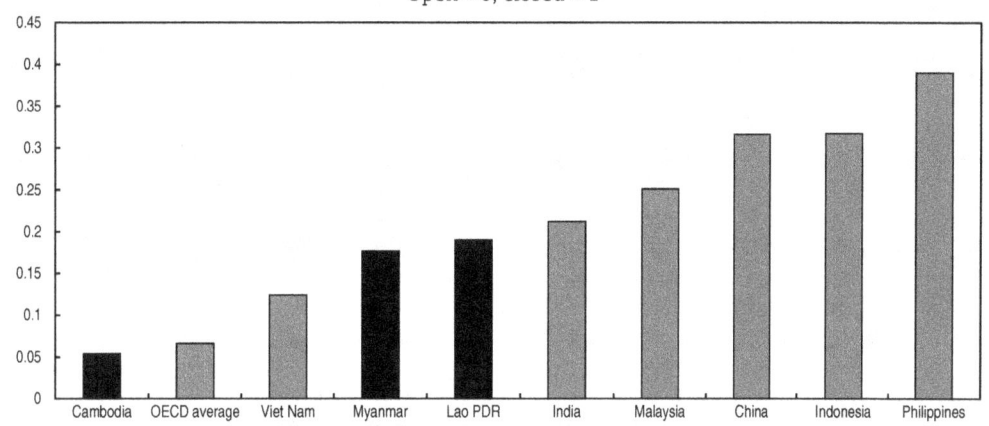

Figure 1.11. **OECD FDI Regulatory Restrictiveness Index scores in Emerging Asia, 2017**
Open = 0, closed = 1

Source: OECD (2018), *OECD FDI Regulatory Restrictiveness Index*.
StatLink https://doi.org/10.1787/888933799853

In Cambodia, the 1994 Law on Investment established the basic regulatory framework governing foreign investment in the country. The law opens all economic sectors to foreign investment and allows foreign stakeholders to own 100% of companies in most sectors, except for state-owned companies and a few sensitive sectors where local participation or prior authorisation is needed. The law forbids any form of discrimination against foreign investors throughout their investment process, while providing incentives in the form of exemption from custom duties and taxes. In 2003, substantial amendments were made to the 1994 law to make investment licensing initiatives simpler, more transparent, predictable, automatic and non-discretional. The Law on Concession, passed in 2007, seeks to promote and facilitate private financing of public infrastructure projects.

Lao PDR's primary law governing foreign investment is the 2016 revised version of the 2009 Law on Investment Promotion. The revised version came into force in April 2017; it enhances investment management by creating the Investment Promotion and Management Committee, streamlines the investment application and approval process, and makes adjustments to the list of promoted sectors and investment incentives. Lao PDR allows foreign investment in all legal sectors, although investments in controlled sectors (those on the negative list) will require strict examination and longer approval. Investments in promoted sectors or in special economic zones (SEZs) are eligible for incentives, including exemptions from profit tax, concession fees, import tariffs and value-added tax. Investors in Lao PDR are allowed to create a 100% foreign-owned company.

> **Box 1.2. Policies supporting foreign direct investment in Cambodia, Lao PDR and Myanmar** *(cont.)*
>
> Myanmar recently introduced several reforms to its regulatory framework for foreign investment. The new Myanmar Investment Law in 2016, which combines the 2013 Citizen Investment Law and the 2012 Foreign Investment Law, allows investment through the Myanmar Investment Commission (MIC) Endorsement in addition to the MIC Permit. MIC-endorsed investors can obtain advantages similar to those of companies with the MIC Permit, in terms of land use, tax exemption, guarantee against confiscation, etc. As the MIC Permit is issued only to investments in certain strategic and controlled areas, the new law can potentially boost FDI in sectors where the MIC Permit is not needed. Another major reform is the approval in 2017 of the new Myanmar Companies Act, which replaces the century-old 1914 Companies Act. The new act allows foreign investors to hold up to 35% of shares in a domestic company without the company losing its local status; previously, a local company had to be 100% owned by Myanmar citizens. This change is considered favourable to foreign investors: they can now enter areas closed to foreigners by investing up to 35% in local companies. Other changes that will also help attract more FDI include reducing the minimum shareholders and the number of directors from two to one, and simplifying the process for company registration.
>
> There is room to strengthen the policy of setting up SEZs to facilitate foreign investments in CLM countries. In Cambodia, the government authorized the creation of SEZs in December 2005 through the Sub-decree on the Establishment and Management of Special Economic Zone. At the same time, a Cambodian Special Economic Zone Board (CSEZB) was established to manage newly created SEZs. To date, the Cambodian government has approved 32 SEZs, with 19 in operation. Cambodia's SEZs have helped attract significant levels of foreign investment that would not have been present otherwise, especially for export-oriented manufacturing investment, because the SEZs provide better infrastructure and lower costs for doing business (ADB, 2015). In Lao PDR, SEZs are used to attract investment in prioritised sectors and to help develop domestic small and medium-sized enterprises (SMEs). Lao PDR's 13 SEZs have different focuses, such as industrial production, tourism, trade and logistics (OECD, 2017a). Myanmar enacted the Special Economic Zone Law in 2014 and now has three SEZs: Kyauk Phyu in Rakhine State, Dawei in the Tanintharyi Region and the Thilawa in Yangon Region. Investment into the Thilawa SEZ accounted for 12.5% of total investment to Myanmar in fiscal year 2014/15.
>
> Regional and bilateral investment-promotion agreements, such as the ASEAN Comprehensive Investment Agreement in 2012, help CLM countries improve the investment environment and attract much-needed FDI. Cambodia signed multiple agreements with China in 2018 to obtain investments, especially in tourism and tourism-related infrastructure projects. In December 2017, Cambodia signed a double-tax avoidance (DTA) agreement with Singapore to clarify taxation rights on all forms of income arising from cross-border business activities. Lao PDR and Myanmar also signed investment agreements and memorandums of understanding with neighbouring countries, especially with China, which has dramatically increased outward investments in the region in recent years.

Myanmar

Myanmar's economic growth is projected to have rebounded to 6.8% in the fiscal year 2017 (ending in March 2018), from 5.9% in the previous year. The recovery of gross exports (in nominal terms), which contracted in 2016, contributed substantially to GDP growth. Consumption also remained buoyant, supported by the continued strong increase in banks' private-sector claims. On the supply side, favourable weather has prompted a rebound in the agriculture sector's output, following a 0.4% contraction in the previous year due to extreme temperatures. Manufacturing PMI, which had been expanding on a month-on-month basis for most of 2017, indicates that offshore orders have been growing at a healthy rate in recent months.

Beginning this year, the government has decided to shift its fiscal year from the current April-March cycle to October-September. As such, there will be an interim six-month period from end-March 2018 to end-September 2018. During this period, the economy is projected to log in 6.9% growth on the expectations that exports will progress further and that agricultural output will continue to recover. The steady improvement in the manufacturing PMI reading from December 2017 to April 2018 is in line with this prognosis. Private consumption will likely be boosted by the 33.0% increase in the minimum wage, applicable to firms with more than ten employees and effective April 2018; this is the first time the mandated wage floor was raised since September 2015. Nonetheless, government spending cannot expand as much in the interim period, given that the requests for supplementary budgets usually made for new projects are halted and pushed to the new fiscal year. One prominent challenge to sustained economic growth is the underdeveloped energy infrastructure, resulting in an unstable power supply. Importing electricity from Lao PDR and India, harnessing natural gas supply and constructing facilities for alternative energy like solar are some proposed stopgap measures as the government targets a 100% electrification rate by 2030. The banking sector's fragility is another source of economic growth friction.

China and India

China

China's economy expanded by 6.9% in 2017, up from 6.7% growth in 2016, the first time it accelerated since 2010. Domestic consumption accounted for much of the GDP growth on the demand side, as it had since 2014 (Figure 1.12). Government spending supported economic growth, fuelled by stronger revenue intake. Private spending also remained robust, as indicated by the 10.2% nominal growth in retail sales of consumer goods in 2017 (not far from the 10.4% growth in 2016), buoyed by the 7.3% increase in real per-capita disposable income, up from 6.3% in 2016. By comparison, investment's contribution to GDP growth declined. Public nominal fixed investment grew by 7.2% in 2017, down from 8.1% in 2016, while private nominal fixed-asset investment grew by 6.0%, almost twice the 3.2% pace the previous year. Finally, the contribution of trade balance has turned positive, after staying in the red in 2015 and 2016. Exporters of manufactures, oils and waxes, crude materials and mineral fuels gained the most in nominal value terms. On the supply side, real value added of agriculture, manufacturing, mining and utilities, and transport-storage services expanded at faster rates. Financial services and WRT growth rates were steady. However, construction grew at a slower pace than in 2016.

Figure 1.12. **Contribution to real GDP growth in China and India, 2015-17**
Percentage points

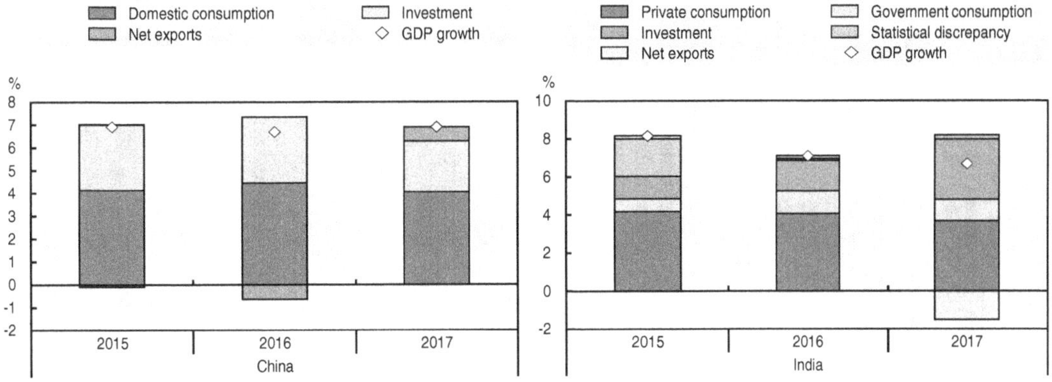

Note: India data refer to fiscal years.
Source: OECD Development Centre calculations based on CEIC data.
StatLink ⟶ https://doi.org/10.1787/888933799872

China's economy is projected to grow by 6.7% in 2018 and 6.4% in 2019. The country's GDP increased by 6.8% in Q1 2018, marginally lower than the 6.9% growth in Q1 2017, but well above the government's 6.5% target for the year. Enduring domestic consumption accounted for much of the aggregate demand push and continues to stay strong. Nominal retail sales increased by 9.8% in Q1 2018, closely tracking the 10.0% growth in the same period last year, and came in at 9.0% in April-May 2018. Consumer confidence touched an all-time high in February 2018 and stayed upbeat through May 2018. The central bank reassured the market of its willingness to stay accommodative, as indicated by the 1.5 percentage point cumulative cut in banks' reserve requirement ratio in April and June 2018. Private fixed investment from January to May 2018 rose by 8.1% YOY (8.9% by the end of Q1 2018), compared with 6.8% from January to May 2017 (7.7% by the end of Q1 2017). Data in April and May 2018 show that goods exports are still gaining steam (Figure 1.13). Manufacturing and non-manufacturing PMIs, which have maintained their expansionary readings through May 2018, reflect this trend (Figure 1.14). The reigning in of shadow banking in the first half of 2018 tightened conditions in financial markets. Especially smaller firms were hard hit and the June reserve requirement cut partially aimed at easing their access to finance. That recent cut was designed to speed up the deleveraging process by promoting debt-equity swaps (Box 1.3). Liquidity provision will be part of the monetary policy arsenal amid slowing economic activity and deleveraging.

Figure 1.13. **Value of goods exports from China and India, 2017-18**

YOY YTD growth

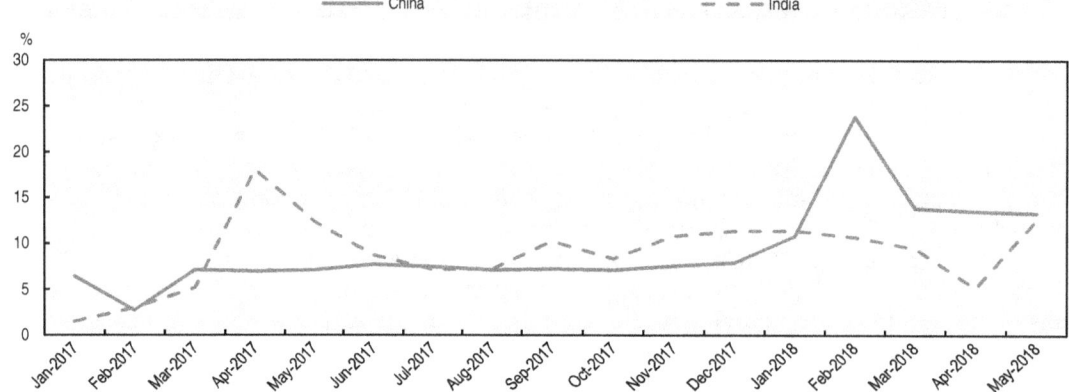

Note: The fiscal year of India is from April to March. Calculations are based on levels data in US dollars.
Source: OECD Development Centre calculations based on CEIC data.
StatLink https://doi.org/10.1787/888933799891

Figure 1.14. **Purchasing Managers' Indices in China and India, 2016-18**

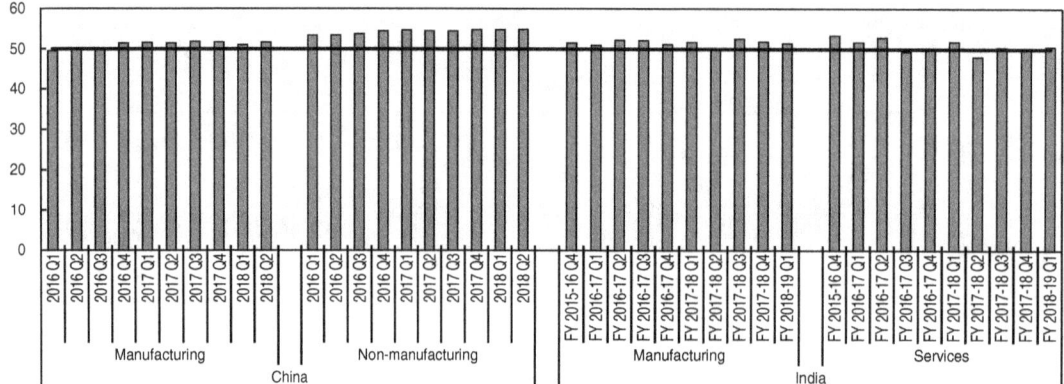

Note: Most recent data are as of May 2018. Index above (below) 50 means expansion (contraction).
Sources: National Bureau of Statistics of China and Markit Economics.
StatLink https://doi.org/10.1787/888933799910

Box 1.3. Changing trends in China's debt

China's overall debt stock is not high by international standards, but its corporate debt relative to gross domestic product (GDP) is higher than in other major economies (Figure 1.15). The Central Economic Work Conference in December 2017 and the Two Sessions in March 2018 designated deleveraging as a policy priority. Corporate debt has peaked off during the past half year or so. The official non-performing loan ratio is still very modest, but excess capacity in many industries and projected slowing growth in the medium term will likely boost that ratio. China is addressing the stock of bad loans by facilitating the write-off as well as the transfer of bad assets to asset management companies, as the 2017 Financial Work Conference suggested. Securitisation is also encouraged. To avoid new bad loans, banks' exposure to a single customer or group has been reduced to a maximum 25% of Tier-1 capital. The country is considering a requirement for multiple banks to jointly issue large loans.

Figure 1.15. **Corporate debt to GDP in China and G7 economies, Q1 2006 – Q4 2017**

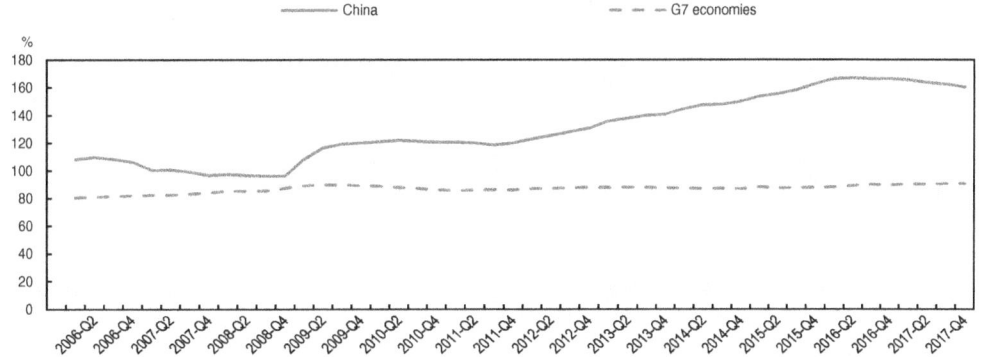

Source: BIS (2018a), "Total credit to non-financial corporations", BIS Statistics (database), https://stats.bis.org/.

StatLink https://doi.org/10.1787/888933799929

Household debt has been rising sharply, though from a low level (Figure 1.16). In 2017, it reached 38% of GDP; this is still a comfortable level by international standards, given that the household sector overall is still a big net saver. Mortgage loan growth has been reined in because of increasingly stringent lending conditions for real estate. However, credit card and consumer loans have been growing rapidly; some of these loans have found their way to the housing market, where they were used for down payment. The way to detect such illegal behaviour is by tracing large fund transfers from multiple accounts to a single one, or by following up on the actual use of such loans.

Figure 1.16. **Household debt to GDP in China and G7 economies, Q1 2006 – Q4 2017**

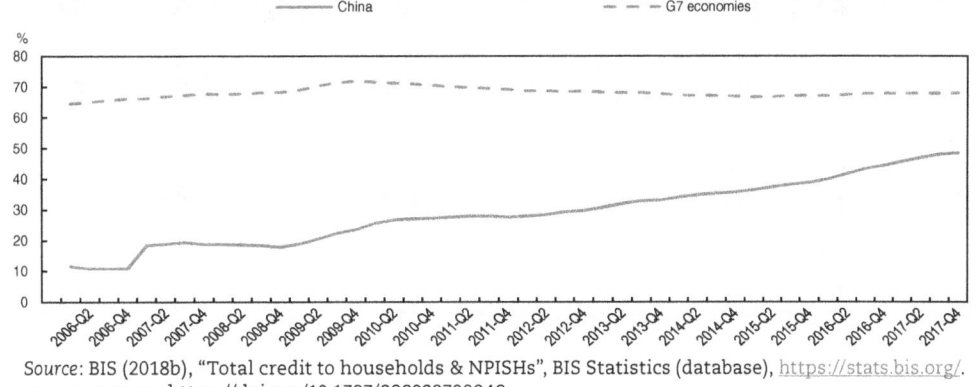

Source: BIS (2018b), "Total credit to households & NPISHs", BIS Statistics (database), https://stats.bis.org/.

StatLink https://doi.org/10.1787/888933799948

India

India's 6.7% GDP growth in fiscal year 2017 (ending March 2018) was slightly slower than the 7.1% rise in 2016, but it indicates that the economy withstood the threats of the lagged effects of demonetisation and the uncertainties brought about by the new goods and services tax relatively well. Major demand-side components grew more moderately, compared with the previous year, but the rates were more than modest. Private consumption growth settled at 6.6%, down from 7.3% in 2017, on slower second-half spending following the introduction of new GST policies. Government consumption grew briskly at 10.9%, feeding off strong budgetary revenue performance, though below the 12.2% the previous year. Fixed investment expansion dropped to 7.6%, from 10.1% the previous year. Infrastructure industries' index growth decelerated, while FDI inflows narrowed slightly. Gross export growth accelerated to 5.6%, from 5.0% the previous year. Growth in offshore demand for services strengthened though growth in shipments of manufactures pulled back. On the supply side, the services sector grew by 7.9%, up from 7.5% the previous year. However, agriculture's growth almost halved to 3.4%, from 6.3% on a higher base in 2016, following droughts in 2015 and 2014. Low crop values, higher operation costs and loan repayment overhang presented difficulties to many small-scale farmers. Manufacturing's growth slowed to 5.7%, from 7.9% the previous year, on limited growth in export sales. Mining's growth slowed to 2.9%, from 13.0% the previous year.

In 2018 and 2019, India's economy is projected to grow by 7.4% and 7.5%, respectively. Personal nominal credit growth accelerated, rising to 20.4% in February 2018, the fastest rate since April 2011 although it has slowed slightly to 17.8% and 19.1% in March 2018 and April 2018, respectively. The robustness in credit growth bodes well for private consumption, as do the accommodative monetary measures through a series of reductions in the mandated liquidity ratio for banks and repo auctions. The turnaround in personal transfers from nationals living overseas, after declining in 2015 and 2016, should boost private spending. However, the decline in consumer confidence entails some apprehension (Figure 1.17). The pace of government spending in 2018 will likely remain close to that of 2017, taking into account the general elections in 2019 and rising revenue growth. On the supply side, the steady PMI expansion suggests that export growth recovery was sustained through March 2018, after contracting in July 2017. The services PMI – which has been on a firmer footing since July-August 2017, when the new GST initiative took effect – also hints that services growth is maintaining momentum. Separately, the higher budget allocation for agriculture, intended to soothe the farm sector's financial distress, could mean better output for the sector this year.

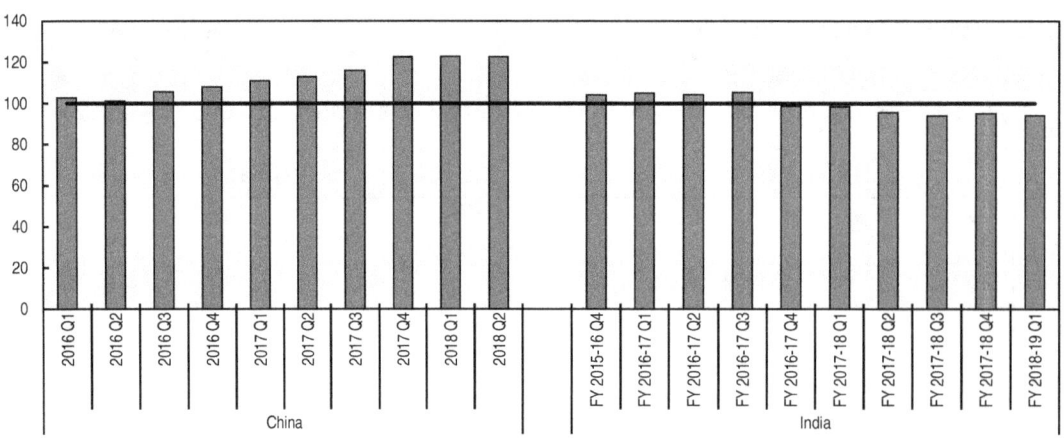

Figure 1.17. **Consumer confidence indices in China and India, 2016-18**

Note: All indices are adjusted to set 100 as neutral confidence point. Most recent data are as of May 2018.
Source: OECD Development Centre calculations based on data from CEIC and national sources.
StatLink https://doi.org/10.1787/888933799967

Headline inflation is firming up in some countries in the region

The consumer price index (CPI) remains mixed among large Southeast Asian economies, although it is generally rising in China and India. In Indonesia, CPI growth averaged 3.3% in the first five months of 2018, lower than the 3.9% growth in the same period in 2017, amid the steady decline in core inflation (Figure 1.18).[2] Prices of processed food, health, transportation, communication and finance continued to lose steam in 2018. The price index of housing, utilities and fuel (HUF) has also eased since peaking in June 2017. By contrast, food prices have risen faster since November 2017, owing to a supply-side glut affecting some raw staples. The government's plan to sustain electricity and fuel price subsidies, together with the rate hikes, should help keep inflation tempered in the near term.

In Malaysia, CPI growth slowed in 2018, averaging 1.7% through May 2018, compared with 4.1% in the same period in 2017. Core inflation was comparably steadier than the headline, although its trend also suggests persistent softening of demand. Of the key components, transport-service cost declined the most. The prices of food, health and education have grown more slowly so far this year, while the growth in HUF prices steadies. The easing of prices can be attributed in part to the fading effects of fuel subsidy rationalisation, the strengthening of the ringgit against the US dollar until April 2018 and the central bank rate tightening in January 2018. Nonetheless, the rise in global oil prices in recent months and the ringgit depreciation against the US dollar since April 2018 could refuel the domestic inflation pressures.

In the Philippines, headline inflation rose to an average of 4.1% (2012=100) and 4.7% (2006=100) in the first five months of 2018, outpacing the inflation rates a year ago of 2.9% (2012=100) and 3.2% (2006=100). Core inflation (2012=100) climbed to 3.2%, from 2.7% a year ago, and its trend indicates the non-transitory nature of the build-up in the cost of goods and services. Prices of alcoholic beverages and tobacco rose by about 17.6% during the period – the highest rise, compared with other CPI baskets. Food and transportation costs have also grown briskly. The passage of the first tranche of the tax reform programme and the prolonged weakness of the peso partly contributed to the rise in prices. The second tax package (containing provisions on tax amnesty and higher motor-vehicle-user charges), the higher global fuel prices and the continued weakness of the currency will likely provide ammunition to inflation in the coming months. The central bank may have raised its policy rate, but the impact of this move may be limited since the push comes largely from the supply side. The reduction in the reserve requirement ratio will also keep the liquidity in the system ample.

In Thailand, headline inflation nudged up to 0.9% on average from January to May 2018, from 0.8% a year ago, with May 2018 data coming in at 1.5%, the fastest rate since January 2017. Core inflation, which excludes fresh foods and energy components, also moved up slightly to 0.7%, from 0.6%, during the same period. The housing price index grew by 1.3% this year, from 0.8% in January-May 2017. The prices of tobacco and alcoholic beverages rose by 6.0%, from 3.5%, during the same period, partly driven by the excise taxes introduced in September 2017. The non-core raw food and energy inflation has increased in the past three months (3.4% in May 2018), after contracting in February 2018, to average 1.5% in 2018 so far, matching the rate in January-May 2017. This recovery in the prices of raw food items seems to result from higher crop supply and limited offshore deals. The baht's healthy appreciation against the US dollar since the beginning of the year through April 2018 helped mitigate the impact of imported inflation. However, with depreciation building up since then, coupled with rising fuel prices in the global market and strong domestic demand, the upside inflation trend will likely persist in the coming months.

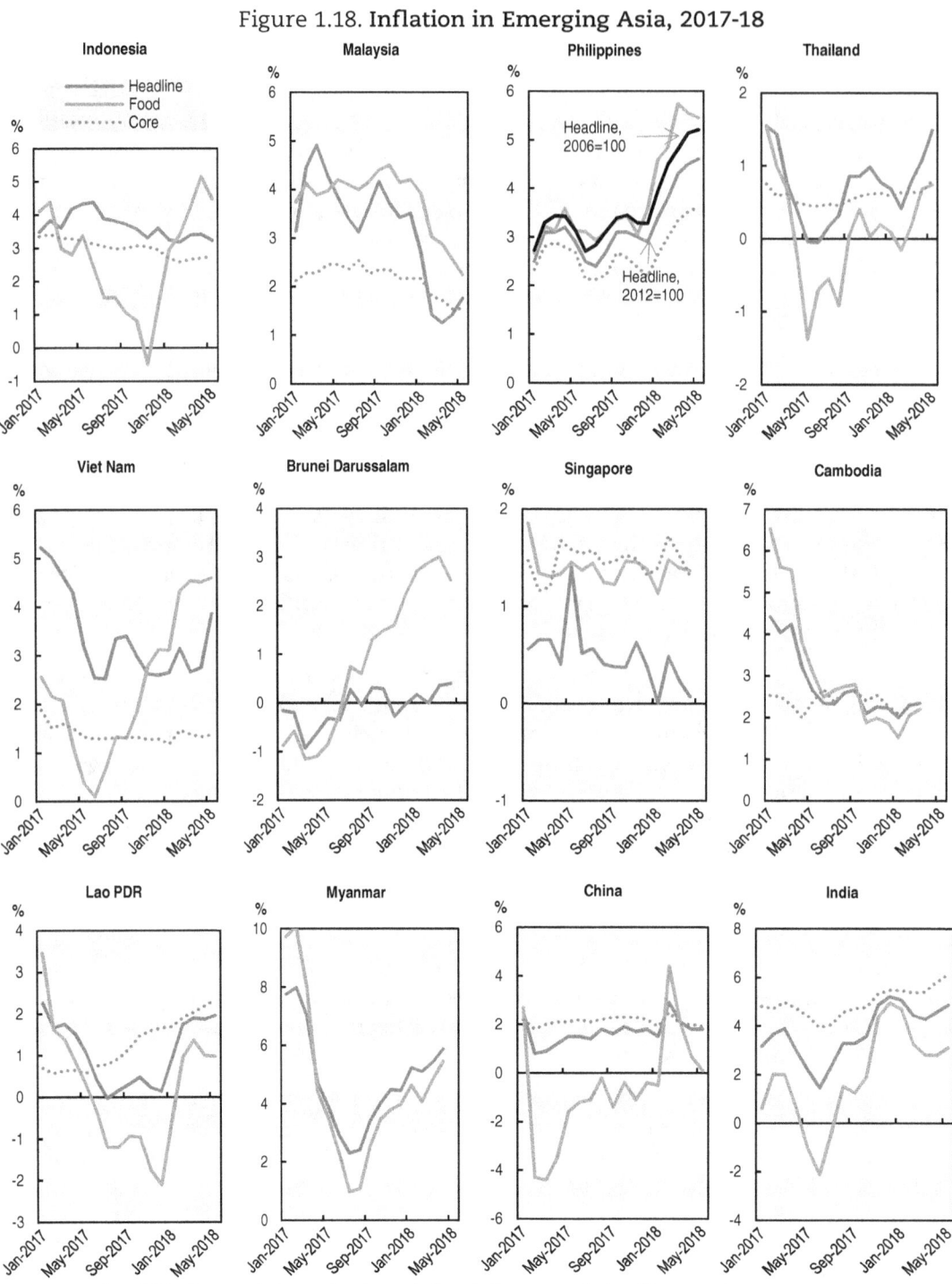

Figure 1.18. **Inflation in Emerging Asia, 2017-18**

Notes: The Philippine Statistics Authority re-indexed the country's headline CPI from 2006=100 to 2012=100. Core inflation of Cambodia refers to CPI excluding Food, Non-Alcoholic Beverage and Energy. Latest data: Brunei Darussalam, Malaysia, Myanmar and Singapore are as of April 2018. Data of Cambodia are as of March 2018.
Source: OECD Development Centre calculations based on CEIC and national sources.
StatLink https://doi.org/10.1787/888933799986

In Viet Nam, headline inflation averaged 3.0% from January to May 2018, slower than the 4.5% posted in the same period in 2017. However, headline inflation had been gradually climbing since December 2017. Transportation and food prices, two of the headline inflation anchors, have risen steadily since June-July 2017. Prices of foodstuff – a separate component from food that has a CPI weight of 22.6% – also rose for the second straight month in May 2018 (0.1% in April and 3.6% in May), after declining from February 2017 to March 2018. Health care and education costs increased markedly, although not as much as in the previous year. Health care costs rose by 27.9%, and education costs by 7.1% in January-May 2018, as the government pushed through with subsidy rationalisation. Core inflation – which excludes food, energy, education and health (based on the national definition) – hovered from 1.2% to 1.5% between April 2017 and May 2018, indicating minimal second-round effects so far. However, near-term prospects point to comparatively more pronounced price growth, given the strong domestic economic expansion and the price pressures in the global commodities markets.

In Brunei Darussalam, headline inflation firmed up to 0.2% on average from January to April 2018, from 0.5% in the same period in 2017, reflecting the recovery in consumer spending. Prices of food and services such as communication, education and restaurants-hotels either rose at a faster pace or reversed the contraction in 2017. By contrast, prices of utilities, transportation, recreation, clothing and housing-related items continued to decline. Improved economic prospects should provide a firmer inflation base in the coming months.

In Singapore, CPI growth from January to April 2018 averaged 0.2%, down from 0.6% in the same period in 2017. CPI growth has fluctuated between 0% and 0.6% from June 2017 to April 2018. Price indices of food, health care and education continued to grow in the past 12 months. By contrast, the HUF price index (26.3% of CPI) contracted by an average of 2.5% in 2018, as of April. Although slightly less deep than the 3.5% reduction in January-April 2017, the drop in the HUF price index was sustained in the past 45 months except in May 2017, when it grew by 0.1% YOY. Transport costs also dipped by an average of 0.6% in March and April 2018, continuing the softening trend that started in April 2017. Core inflation (which takes out the costs of private road transport and accommodation, but includes food and energy in the case of Singapore) rose slightly to 1.5% this year through April 2018, from 1.4% in January-April 2017. However, the trend starting in May 2017 has been treading downwards. The 1 percentage point increase in the buyer's stamp duty rate on a residential property's value in excess of SGD 1 million (Singapore dollars), announced in February 2018, may further dampen housing demand and housing prices. However, higher global oil prices are expected to continue pushing up prices.

Headline inflation in Cambodia in Q1 2018, which came in at 2.2%, is markedly slower than the 4.0% in the same period in 2017. Food inflation dipped to 1.9% during the period, from 5.4% a year earlier, due to subdued crop prices after a bumper harvest. The average growth of health costs decelerated, from 1.9% to 1.2%, as did that of transportation costs, from 4.6% to 3.1%. The communication price index declined for the sixth straight month; this was the 16th time in the past 18 months that it contracted. The steady decline in communications costs (-1.2% in January-April 2018) can be attributed to tighter competition in the domestic telecommunications industry, which has made mobile phones and data subscription packages more affordable. By comparison, the HUF price index is climbing gradually, presumably indicating an easing of the housing supply glut. Nonetheless, the government's decision to cut electricity rates beginning April 2018 could push back the HUF price trend.

In Lao PDR, average headline inflation settled at 1.7% in January-May 2018, about the same rate in the same period the previous year. However, the trend has been rising since July 2017, when inflation bottomed at 0%. CPI growth was largely influenced by the firming up of food and transport price indices in recent months – i.e. since February 2018 in the case of food, and since July 2017 for transportation. By comparison, average core inflation (which excludes food and fuel) more than tripled, to 2.0% in January-May 2018, from 0.6% in January-May 2017. The price indices of HUF, clothing, alcoholic beverages and tobacco, health and telecommunications grew at a faster pace in the first five months of 2018 than in the comparable period in 2017. In the near term, rising oil prices and the minimum wage increase are two upside risks to inflation. However, the anticipated improvement in the agriculture harvest, resulting from government support and better weather, provides an offsetting factor.

Headline inflation in Myanmar averaged 5.4% from January to April 2018, lower than the 6.9% in the same period in 2017. Nonetheless, headline inflation in the country had been increasing since bottoming in July 2017. The U-shaped path of food prices strongly influenced the CPI: food prices rose to 5.5% in April 2018, from 1.0% in July 2017, after averaging 9.3% in Q1 2017. Prices of alcoholic beverages and tobacco have buoyed up inflation this year; the price index average growth rose to 19.4% in 2018, from 2.4% in the same period in 2017. The tighter implementation of the tax stamp policy has accelerated the uptick in the cost of alcohol and tobacco from 1.2% in August 2017 to 25.1% in February 2018, before receding to 19.4% and 13.3% in the next two months. The robust rise in the price indices of communications services and HUF also boosted CPI growth. Communication-services cost grew by an average of 9.4% this year, after contracting by 2.3% around the same time last year, while HUF grew by 7.1%, up from 6.4%. On the other hand, clothing and transport prices have risen less this year so far, compared with 2017.

In China, headline CPI growth strengthened in early 2018. The food price index is a notable inflation anchor in 2018, growing by an average of 1.8% in February-May 2018 after exiting the contractionary cycle that stretched from February 2017 to January 2018. Core inflation – defined to exclude food and energy prices – has also risen marginally, to 2.1% in January-May 2018, from 2.0% in January-May 2017. The health care price index climbed from 5.4% to 5.6%. The gradual removal of mandated price ceilings on certain health services has allowed prices to adjust more flexibly to market forces. The anticipated mild weakening of domestic demand growth and the continued rationalisation of subsidies on certain goods (like new energy vehicles) is a downside inflation factor moving forward. However, the risk of a broader tariff schedule on imported goods and higher crude oil prices is an upside inflation driver.

In India, headline inflation averaged 4.6% in January-May 2018, outpacing the 3.2% recorded in the same months in 2017. A broad set of factors influenced this increase. During the same period, average core inflation – which removes food and beverages, pan (betel leaves), tobacco and intoxicants, and fuel and light – grew by 5.6%, from 4.7% a year ago. Product-level data show that the food price index rose by 3.3%, from 0.8%. Similarly, fuel and light prices increased by 6.3%, from 4.9%; housing prices grew by 8.4%, from 4.9%; the prices of pan-tobacco and intoxicants rose by 7.7%, from 6.2%; and clothing prices climbed by 5.1%, from 4.5%. The increased floor price of crops under the government's support mechanism in FY 2018-19, as well as increased import tariffs on some food products, will likely buoy food inflation in the near term. Relatively higher global oil prices this year is another inflation upside factor.

Central banks have started to raise policy rates but are using other tools to maintain liquidity

Until October 2017, the policy rate actions of regional central banks indicated comfort with relatively low interest rates. However, sentiments seem to have swung in the opposite direction since then. Bank Negara Malaysia (BNM), for example, raised its policy rate by 25 basis points (bps), from 3.0% to 3.25% in January 2018, to prevent risks due to prolonged low interest rates (Figure 1.19). Bangko Sentral ng Pilipinas (BSP) raised the overnight reverse repo rate by 50 bps cumulatively in May 2018 and June 2018, to 3.5%. Bank Indonesia (BI) increased its seven-day repo rate three times by a total of 100 bps in May-June 2018 to 5.25%. The Reserve Bank of India (RBI) likewise raised its policy rate by 25 bps, to 6.25% in June 2018. The decisions of BSP, BI and RBI to raise rates were mainly influenced by the relative weakness in domestic currencies as well as the build-up of price pressures as indicated in the official central bank reports. Prior to the recent policy rate actions, these central banks last raised their policy rates in 2014 (i.e. RBI in January 2014, BNM in July 2014, BSP in September 2014 and BI in November 2014).

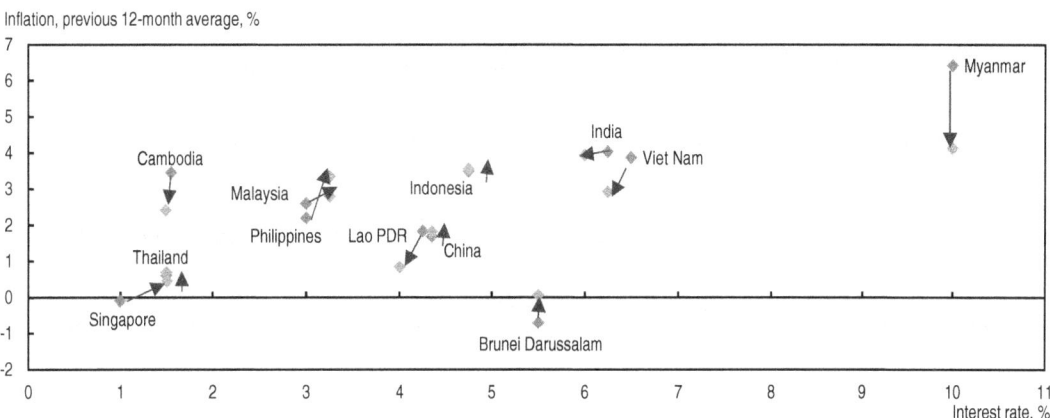

Figure 1.19. **Evolution of inflation and benchmark interest rates**

Notes: The policy and benchmark interest rates used in the chart are as follows: prime lending rate (Brunei Darussalam), saving deposit rate as provided by IMF (Cambodia), nominal lending rate ≤1 year (China), repo rate (India), BI 7-day reverse repo rate (Indonesia), BOL short-term lending rate (Lao PDR), overnight policy rate (Malaysia), central bank 1-year fixed deposit rate (Myanmar), reverse repo rate (Philippines), monthly average of SIBOR (Singapore), repo rate (Thailand) and refinancing rate (Viet Nam). Annualised inflation pertains to the 12-month average of monthly inflation rates up to the latest data. Latest data: Brunei Darussalam, Malaysia, Myanmar and Singapore are as of April 2018. Data of Cambodia are as of March 2018.
Source: OECD Development Centre calculations based on data from CEIC and national sources.
StatLink ⎘ https://doi.org/10.1787/888933800005

To buttress the impact of the policy rate hikes on domestic demand, some central banks used other tools to inject liquidity into their respective financial systems. This stance appears to be an attempt to isolate the direct monetary policy impact on exchange rate, inflation and domestic credit flows. Such policy mix conveys that central banks, though wary of the exchange rate and inflation dynamics, are not keen on stifling domestic credit flow especially at a time when some national governments plan to roll out large infrastructure projects.

For instance, in February 2018, BSP cut the reserve requirement ratio (RRR) – imposed on universal-commercial banks and non-bank financial institutions with quasi-banking functions – by 100 bps, from 20.0% to 19.0%, effective the following month. Another 100-bps RRR cut was announced in May 2018 to lower the mandated RRR ratio to 18.0%. BSP hinted that it may lower the ratio further, to a single digit, if circumstances permit. Before this year's actions, BSP last reduced the mandated RRR for universal-commercial banks in April 2012; the ratio has never dropped below 12.0% since 1980 (the earliest data point available).

Similarly, in January 2018, BI lowered the average daily RRR on rupiah deposits by 50 bps, from 5.0% to 4.5%, although it kept the two-week RRR at 6.5%. BI also introduced new measures: the macroprudential intermediation ratio (MIR) and the macroprudential liquidity buffer (MLB) in lieu of the loan to funding ratio, financing to deposit ratio and secondary reserve requirement, effective from July to October 2018 to buoy bank lending. MIR will include some generic securities and *shari'a* securities held by banks in the calculation of the loan-to-funding ratio (for conventional banks) and the financing-to-deposit ratio (for *shari'a* commercial banks and business units).[3] MLB, on the other hand, allows conventional and *shari'a* banks to sell 2.0% of securities held as secondary reserves to the central bank through a repo arrangement. Moreover, to support economic activity, BI adjusted the stages and limits applicable to liquidate loans; and relaxed regulations concerning the loan-to-value and financing-to-value ratios for properties and the number of credit facilities available through the pre-order mechanism.

In Viet Nam, liquidity tightening in the interbank market prompted the State Bank of Vietnam (SBV) to lower the open market operations rate by 25 bps, from 5.0% to 4.75%, in January 2018 – the first time it has done so since 2014. In July 2017, SBV likewise cut the discount and refinancing rates by 25 bps to support economic activity. Recent monetary policy actions of SBV have focused on facilitating stability in the foreign currency market while it continues to bolster its foreign exchange reserves.

Outside Southeast Asia, the People's Bank of China (PBOC) has shown its willingness to calibrate its other monetary tools both ways to manage risks to domestic activity. On the one hand, PBOC raised its 7-day, 14-day and 28-day reverse repurchase rates by 5 to 10 bps (essentially symbolic) to mirror the US Fed's action from December 2017 to March 2018. On the other hand, PBOC cut the RRR by 1 percentage point in April, effective the same month, and then again by 50 bps in June 2018 effective in July 2018. Conditional RRR cuts announced in September 2017 to promote financial inclusion became effective in January 2018. PBOC released another CNY 400 billion (Chinese Yuan renminbi) through its medium-term lending facility at the beginning of 2018. In March 2018, RBI announced its own capital injection, amounting to INR 1 billion (Indian rupees) spread in four equal tranches of variable rate term repo auctions. In October 2017, RBI also lowered its statutory liquidity ratio (SLR) by 50 bps, the third time the RBI did so in 2017. Aggregate SLR reduction totalled 125 bps in 2017.

Current account balances remain moderate, except for those of oil exporters

The strong recovery in global oil prices has boosted the current account positions of the two oil exporters in Emerging Asia: Brunei Darussalam and Malaysia. However the current account balances (CAB) of other Emerging Asian countries have moderated in 2017 (Figure 1.20). In the coming years, the current account balances of most regional economies will moderate further. The current account surplus of the ASEAN countries is forecast to drop from 2.4% of GDP in 2017 to 1.8% in 2018, and to 1.5% in 2019. The current account surplus of the Emerging Asian countries will narrow from 0.8% of GDP in 2017 to 0.5% in 2018, and 0.3% in 2019.

Indonesia's current account remained in deficit at 1.7% of GDP in 2017 though smaller than the gap in 2016 of 1.8% of GDP. The services trade deficit, as well as net outflows in factor income and transfer payments, offset the strong performance from goods exports. Indonesia's CAB-to-GDP ratio is expected to come in at around -1.8% in 2018 and -1.7% in 2019, respectively. Malaysia's CAB-to-GDP ratio widened in 2017 to 3.0% in 2017 from 2.4% in 2016; this was due in part to the oil price recovery and strong offshore sales of other products such as manufactures, machineries and transport equipment, which helped boost Malaysia's goods exports growth. This surplus, however, is expected to narrow to 2.4% of GDP in 2018 and to 2.2% of GDP in 2019. The Philippines' current account entered into the negative zone in 2016 and stayed in the red in 2017. While gross export growth recovered in 2017, gross import growth stayed robust mainly due to domestic demand for raw materials and fuel. Meanwhile, growth in secondary income, which includes remittances of workers overseas, steadied. The CAB-to-GDP ratio of the Philippines is projected to widen from -0.8% in 2017 to -1.2% in 2018 and to -1.4% in 2019. Progress in the government's infrastructure investment plan will likely boost capital import growth. The strength of service exports through business process outsourcing receipts as well as continued inflow of overseas workers' remittances could provide some buffer for the country's CAB. Thailand's current account surplus stayed healthy in 2017, at 10.6% of GDP, supported by strong export growth in both goods and services. Gross export growth strengthened in 2017 as does the growth in income transfers. But, import growth across commodity baskets also surged, led by fuel, raw and intermediate goods, and capital goods. Thailand's CAB-to-GDP ratio is projected to narrow to 10.5% in 2018 and 8.5% in 2019 in anticipation of relatively more modest export growth coupled by brisk growth in goods imports supporting domestic investment. Viet Nam's current account remained in surplus in 2017, at 2.9% of GDP, though nudged down from 2016. Exports and imports of goods grew at considerable pace in 2017. However, the outflow in primary and secondary income has picked up more briskly than the inflow. Viet Nam's CAB-to-GDP ratio is forecast to remain at 2.9% in 2018 before declining marginally to 2.8% in 2019.

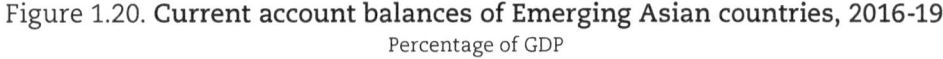

Figure 1.20. **Current account balances of Emerging Asian countries, 2016-19**
Percentage of GDP

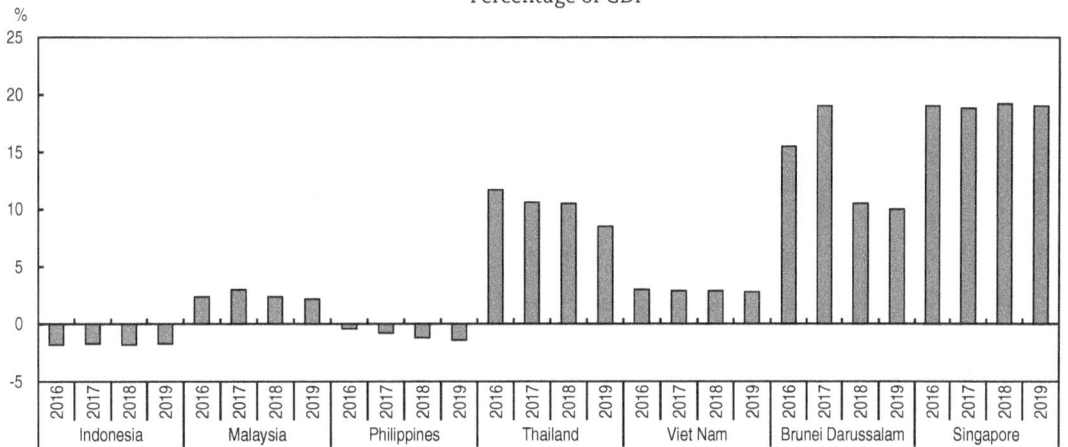

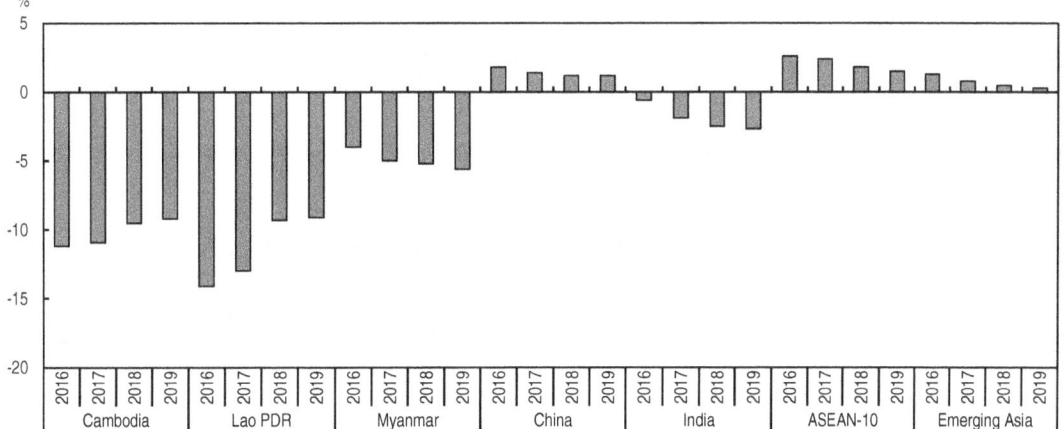

Note: The cut-off date for data used is 18 June 2018. The weighted averages are used for ASEAN average and Emerging Asia average. Data of India and Myanmar follow fiscal years. For Myanmar, 2018 refers to the interim 6-month period from April 2018 to September 2018 while 2019 refers to fiscal year starting October 2018 to September 2019. The projections of China, India and Indonesia are based on the OECD Economic Outlook No. 103 (database).
Source: OECD Development Centre, MPF-2018 (Medium-term Projection Framework); CEIC; country sources and ADB (2018a).

StatLink https://doi.org/10.1787/888933800024

Brunei Darussalam's CAB-to-GDP ratio improved substantially to 19.0% in 2017 from 15.5% in 2016 benefitting from the recovery in receipts from exports of mineral fuels (e.g. crude oil and natural gas). However, the country's future current account surplus is projected to decline to 10.5% of GDP in 2018 and to 10.0% of GDP in 2019 as the impact of oil price increase wanes. Singapore continued to register relatively high CAB-to-GDP ratio in 2017 at 18.8%, almost unchanged from the previous year. Oil price recovery boosted the nominal value of exports of and imports of mineral fuels of Singapore, which hosts large refinery businesses. Growth in primary income receipts has likewise stayed robust. Singapore's CAB-to-GDP ratio is estimated to remain large in 2018 and 2019 at 19.2% and 19.0% respectively.

Cambodia's CAB-to-GDP ratio stayed negative but is estimated to have slightly improved to -10.9% in 2017 from -11.2% in 2016. Trade deficit in goods has narrowed in 2017 while trade surplus in services rose. The widening of net income inflows deficit was likewise offset by the increase in current transfer net position. The CAB-to-GDP ratio of Cambodia is projected to come in at -9.5% in 2018 and -9.2% in 2019. In Lao PDR, smaller gross trade deficit and higher current transfer position have also resulted in the tightening of the current account gap to about 13% of GDP in 2017 from 14.1% of GDP in 2016. Considering the promising electricity export deals that the country has entered into recently, the CAB-to-GDP ratio is projected to be about -9.3% in 2018 and -9.1% in 2019. By comparison, Myanmar's CAB-to-GDP ratio is estimated to have regressed to -5.0% in fiscal year 2017 from -4.0% in fiscal year 2016. While gross exports have recovered, gross imports have posted much higher growth. In particular, the value of imported consumer and intermediate goods had increased steeply. The CAB-to-GDP ratio of Myanmar is forecasted to decline further to -5.2% in 2018 and to -5.6% in 2019.

In 2017, China's current account surplus stood at 1.4% of GDP, down from 1.8% of GDP in 2016 and less than half of what it was a decade ago. Nominal gross exports rose 10.2% in 2017 after contracting by 6.9% in 2016. But, this was more than matched by the nominal gross import growth which logged in at 13.9% in 2017 from -3.0% in 2016. The inbound shipment value of a number of products has risen, pronouncedly especially fuel, crude materials and primary products. The CAB-to-GDP of China is expected to settle at 1.2% in 2018 and 2019. India's current account deficit widened in fiscal year 2017 to 1.9% of GDP from 0.6% of GDP in fiscal year 2016. The deterioration in goods trade balance has outweighed the gains in services trade (in the form of software and technical support services). In particular, growth in the value of imports of petroleum and related products, non-monetary gold, precious stones and other metals for jewelleries has accelerated markedly during the period. In 2018 and 2019, India is forecast to log in a CAB-to-GDP ratio of -2.5% and -2.7%, respectively.

FDI inflows remain strong for most Emerging Asian countries

FDI inflows to Emerging Asia recovered strongly in 2017 after a significant fall in 2016 (Figure 1.21). FDI inflows in 2017 increased by about 10.0% for the ASEAN-10 countries, and by 1.0% for ASEAN-10 plus China and India. FDI inflows to ASEAN continued to rise, owing to robust regional economic growth, strong domestic demand, growing trade and the announcement of large government-sponsored projects. EU and intra-ASEAN FDI are the largest sources of capital in the region; the United States and Japan remain major players, although their influence is declining. Chinese investments have been rising in recent years, targeting mainly finance, wholesale and retail trade, transportation and the real estate sector (ASEAN, 2017).

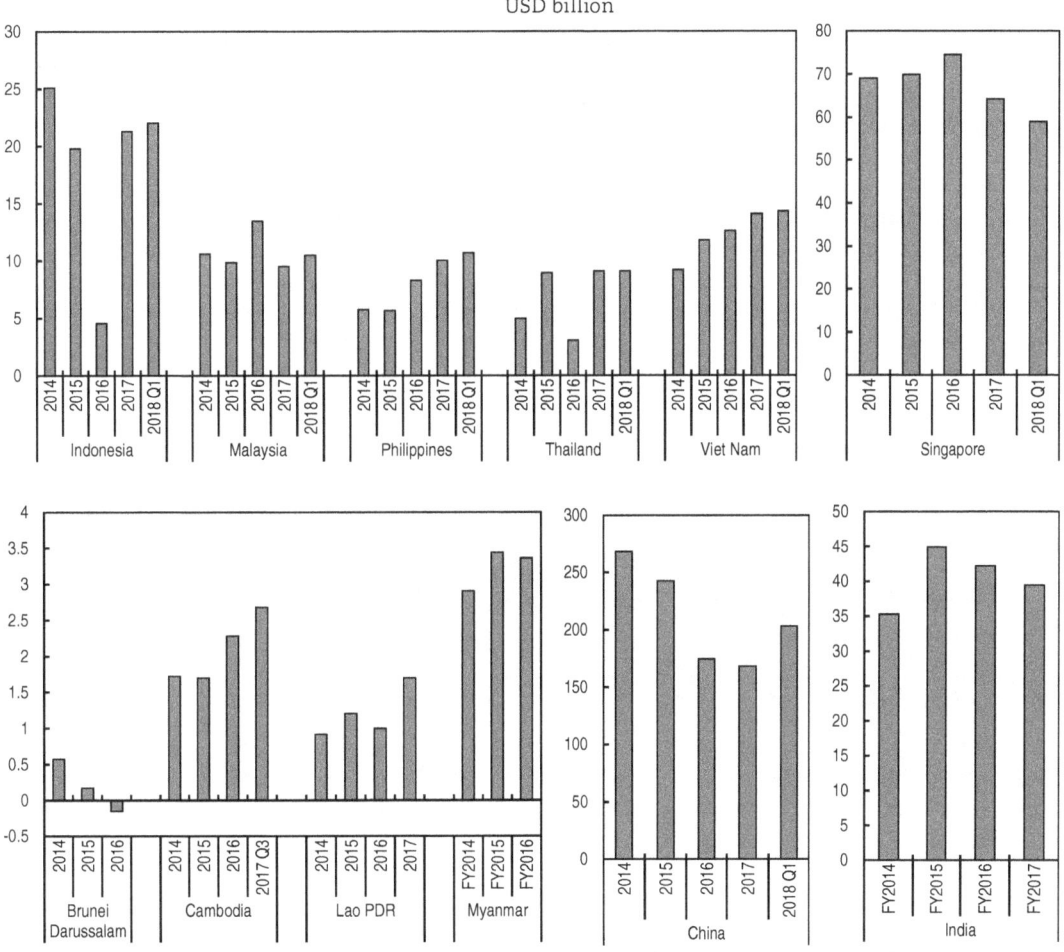

Figure 1.21. **Foreign direct investment in Emerging Asian countries, 2014-18**
USD billion

Notes: Myanmar and India follow fiscal years ending in March the following year. Quarterly data are annualised (i.e. four-quarter sum as of the period indicated). The asset/liability principle is followed in the presentation of FDI data. FDI inflows data refer to foreign placements minus foreign withdrawals (Balance of Payments liability side).
Source: OECD Development Centre calculations based on CEIC data, national sources and IMF (2018b), International Financial Statistics (database).
StatLink ⟶ https://doi.org/10.1787/888933800043

FDI inflows to Indonesia recovered to US 21.3 billion in 2017 after dropping to USD 4.5 billion in 2016 as concerns rose over possible US policy changes under the new administration and over domestic uncertainties. These issues led to capital outflows in the last quarter of the year. Despite a small decline, FDI inflows to Malaysia remained strong in 2017, reaching USD 9.5 billion. Service activities overtook manufacturing as the major FDI destination, attracting more than 40.0% of total investments, followed by 35.0% for manufacturing, and 22.0% for mining and quarrying. In the Philippines, FDI inflows rose from USD 8.3 billion in 2016 to USD 10 billion in 2017, indicative of well-grounded investor confidence presumably due to optimistic economic prospects and the strong infrastructure campaign. The energy sector attracted 42.0% of the inflows, followed by manufacturing at 35.0%, and real estate at 7.6%. Thailand's FDI inflows increased to USD 9.1 billion in 2017 from USD 3.1 billion in 2016. The financial and insurance activities obtained the biggest share in inflows, followed by manufacturing and real estate activities. From USD 12.6 billion in 2016, FDI inflows to Viet Nam reached USD 14.1 billion in 2017, which was only below Indonesia and Singapore among its ASEAN peers. Manufacturing and real estate have been the largest FDI recipients in Viet Nam.

FDI in Brunei Darussalam fell in 2016 due to weak oil prices, but the 2017 figure (which has not yet been released) is expected to be higher. A substantial chunk of FDI has gone to the mining and quarrying sectors in the last few years although the government is keen on making other industries attractive to foreign investors. Singapore received FDI amounting to USD 64.2 billion in 2017, lower than the USD 74.5 billion in 2016, but still the largest among ASEAN economies. The sectors of financial and insurance services, wholesale and retail trade, and manufacturing attract most of the foreign capital coming to the city-state. FDI inflows to the CLM countries were relatively small but have been increasing steadily. For Cambodia, China has been the dominant foreign investor for a long time; China is primarily interested in Cambodia's service sector, especially tourism. In Lao PDR, FDI inflows are mainly allocated to the energy and mining sectors. By comparison, FDI inflows in Myanmar, are largely channelled to manufacturing, real estate development, energy and agriculture.

China's FDI inflows reached USD 168.2 billion in 2017, slightly below its level in 2016. The moderation in foreign capital inflow in recent years can be associated with excess capacity and rising production costs in manufacturing and relatively limited opportunities for foreign investors in several service industries. The recently released negative list will open up opportunities. Foreign investments in China mainly go to manufacturing, information and communication technology, real estate, leasing and commercial service, and wholesale and retail trade. FDI flows to India dropped slightly to USD 39.4 billion in fiscal year 2017 and the general trend shows a mixed picture recently, somehow related to pace of domestic reforms.

Capital markets adjust to tighter liquidity and the downward pull on asset prices

Local currency bond yields in Emerging Asia have generally risen since December 2017, largely following the US lead, while yields of benchmark bonds of major European economies continue to move sideways, with the short end remaining below zero in many cases. In the last five months through end-May 2018, one-year bond yields have climbed the most in the Philippines, compared with other Emerging Asian economies. Ten-year bond yields have risen the most in Indonesia. Extending the time horizon two years further shows that the rise in yields has been most persistent in the Philippines, despite the currency depreciation and the central bank's loose monetary stance. Between May 2016 and June 2018, trading in the country's secondary market saw one-year bond yields rise by about 2.7 percentage points, while ten-year bond yields rose by 2.0 percentage points. These increases were fuelled in part by the government's push to substantially increase operational and infrastructure spending, as well as by faster inflation growth in recent months. In China and Viet Nam, 1-year bond yields have been on a downward path largely due to accommodative stance of monetary policy. 10-year bond yields in Viet Nam have risen, associated with strong demand for long-term funds, while yields in China are falling, related to business performance. In Thailand, short-term yields have moved largely sideways, whereas long-term yields are rising. In India, both the short- and long-term yields declined for about four weeks since the beginning of March 2018, but have bounced back up in the three months that followed.

The term spreads (i.e. the difference between ten-year bond yields and one-year bond yields) in Emerging Asian economies have mostly risen from September 2017 to March 2018, but have fallen from April to June 2018 as expectations of short-term inflation pressures in a number of countries build up (Figure 1.22). The market is also pricing in liquidity tightening in the next few quarters, even though many central banks have kept an accommodative stance so far through the use of non-traditional tools. By comparison, the US yield curve steepened about two months before the end of 2017, but the trend has reversed to flattening afterwards, with the short end rising to levels comparable to that in June 2008. Moreover, the increases in US bond yields have outpaced the hikes in Emerging Asia, resulting in narrower premium spreads both in the short and long ends.

Figure 1.22. **Benchmark bond yield and term spreads in the United States and Emerging Asia, 2012-18**
Percentage points

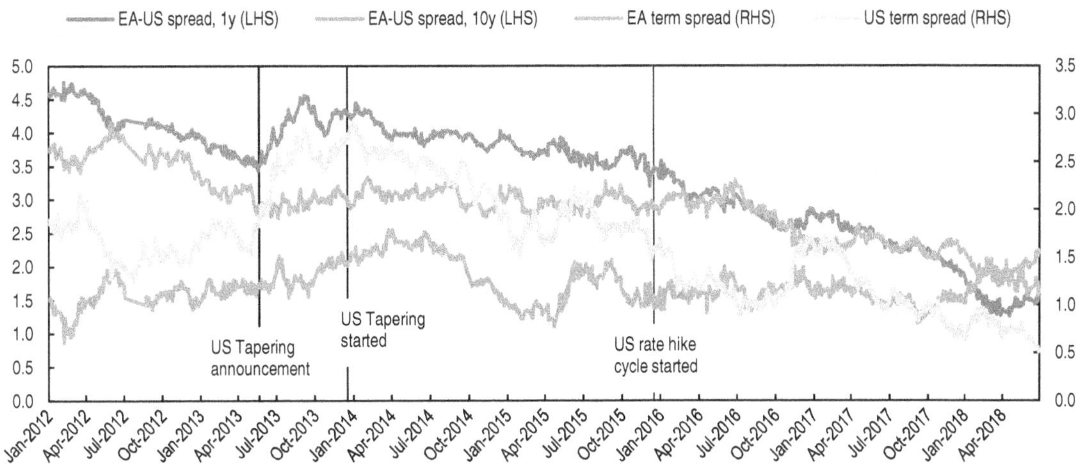

Note: Emerging Asia = simple average of government bond yields of China, India, Indonesia, the Philippines, Singapore, Thailand and Viet Nam. Term spread = 10-year yield minus 1-year yield. RHS means right hand scale and LHS means left hand scale. Most recent data are as of 29 June 2018.
Source: OECD Development Centre based on Fusion Media Ltd. (2018), www.investing.com.
StatLink https://doi.org/10.1787/888933800062

Portfolio and other investment (POI) inflows data in 2018 Q1, where available, suggest that Emerging Asia remains attractive to foreign secondary market investors and that the amount of net withdrawal (as in the case of the Philippines) has remained benign. In 2017, POI inflows in Emerging Asian economies have largely picked up from 2016, riding on concerted GDP growth pick-up globally, improvement in global trade picture and the absence of monetary policy surprises in advanced economies (Figure 1.23). The continued dwindling of premium spreads, however, can negatively affect capital flows, especially in light of the hefty borrowing programme outlined by the US government and the drag to global liquidity (mainly in US dollars) when major central banks recalibrate their balance sheets. Credit-default swap (CDS) spreads have somewhat risen since mid-January 2018, reflecting the return of market volatility, increasing cost of credit and broadening global risks to corporate revenue streams and asset prices (Figure 1.24).

In equity markets, agitations arose largely from uncertainty in US monetary policy, tensions in the Middle East and broadening trade protectionism. These concerns sent stock price indices reeling downwards after touching historic highs from November 2017 to April 2018 (Figure 1.25). Data through end-June 2018 show that the Philippines Stock Exchange index had seen the steepest decline this year among major Emerging Asian stock indices, dropping 15.9% YTD and 20.6% since peak to pin the bellwether index to its lowest level since the first two trading days of January 2017. Similarly, the Shanghai Stock Exchange composite index declined 13.9% YTD and 20.0% since peak in the first six months of the year, given the growing overseas threats to corporate earnings. The main stock indices of Indonesia, Lao PDR, Malaysia and Myanmar lost between 0.6% and 9.5% YTD and between 5.5% and 14.2% since peak of their values during the period. The Vietnam Ho Chi Minh Stock index, which was growing robustly until the first two weeks of April 2018 (reflecting the economic growth in the past three quarters), has likewise slumped by 2.4% YTD and 20.2% since peak as of end-June 2018. Elsewhere in the region, sentiments in the equity markets in Cambodia, India, Singapore and Thailand are also pessimistic. Nevertheless, the relative valuation of equities in some Emerging Asian markets is comparably higher than in many markets outside the region (Box 1.4).

Figure 1.23. **Portfolio and other investment inflows in Emerging Asian countries, 2014-18**
USD billion

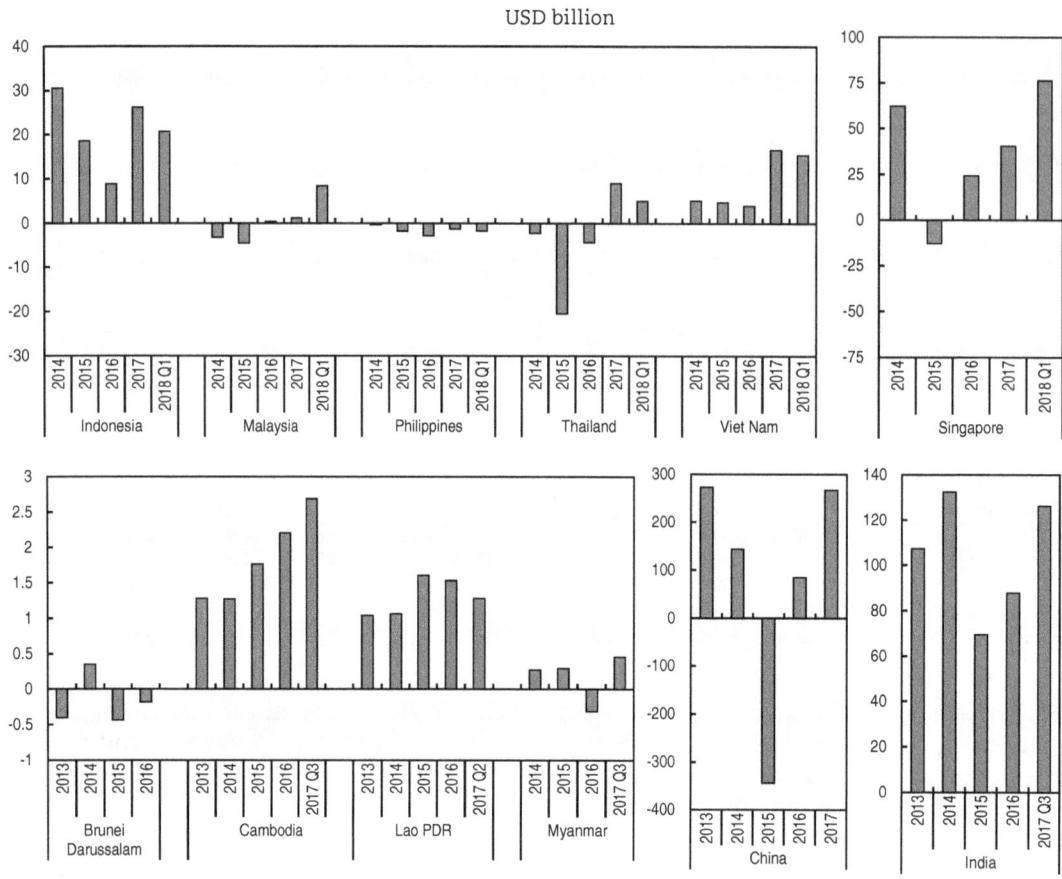

Note: Data of India and Myanmar follow fiscal years. Quarterly data are annualised, i.e. 4-quarter moving sum. Malaysia's data only pertain to portfolio investment. Portfolio and other investment inflows data refer to foreign placements minus foreign withdrawals (Balance of Payments liability side).
Source: OECD Development Centre calculations based on data from CEIC, IMF and national sources.
StatLink ⟶ https://doi.org/10.1787/888933800081

Figure 1.24. **Credit Default Swap (5-year senior) in ASEAN-5 and China, 2015-18**
Mid-spread, basis points

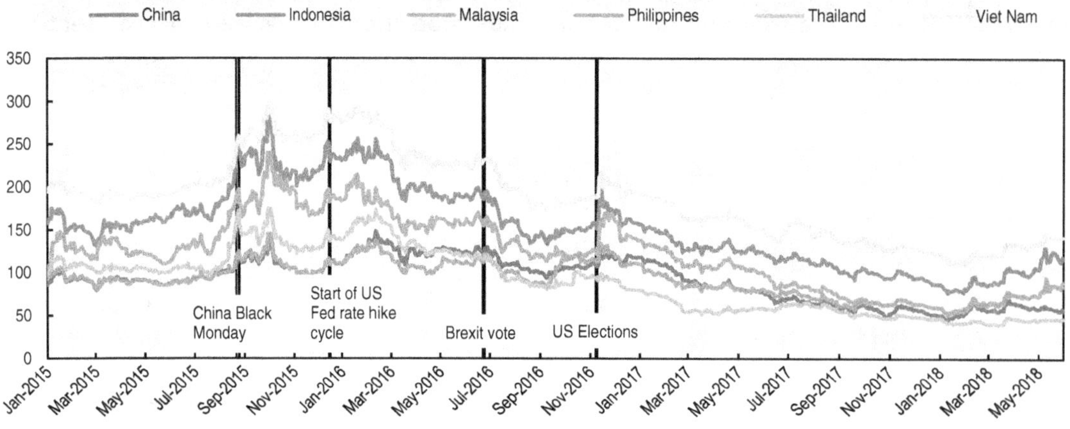

Note: Most recent data are as of 31 May 2018.
Source: OECD Development Centre based on data from Datastream.
StatLink ⟶ https://doi.org/10.1787/888933800100

Figure 1.25. **Equity market returns in Emerging Asia, 2016-18**

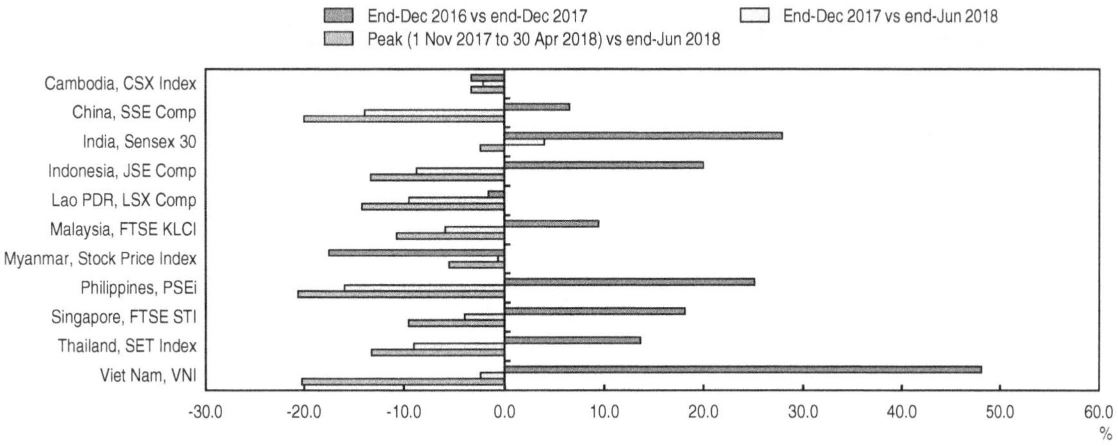

- End-Dec 2016 vs end-Dec 2017
- End-Dec 2017 vs end-Jun 2018
- Peak (1 Nov 2017 to 30 Apr 2018) vs end-Jun 2018

[Bar chart showing equity market returns for: Cambodia, CSX Index; China, SSE Comp; India, Sensex 30; Indonesia, JSE Comp; Lao PDR, LSX Comp; Malaysia, FTSE KLCI; Myanmar, Stock Price Index; Philippines, PSEi; Singapore, FTSE STI; Thailand, SET Index; Viet Nam, VNI. X-axis: -30.0 to 60.0 %]

Note: Data are as of 29 June 2018.
Source: OECD Development Centre based on Fusion Media Ltd. (2018), www.investing.com.
StatLink ⇒ https://doi.org/10.1787/888933800119

Box 1.4. Relative valuation of the stock price of companies in Emerging Asia

Despite the price corrections, however, a number of Emerging Asian stock markets are still among the most expensive globally. The price-earnings (P/E) ratio is a metric that compares the stock price of the company as traded and the declared corporate earnings per share. Estimates of the standard P/E and cyclically adjusted P/E ratios of Keimling (2018) as of 31 May 2018, shows that equity markets in India, the Philippines, Malaysia and Indonesia are in the 70th percentile or above in either or both measures out of the 40 countries examined. In addition, the stock market of Viet Nam, which was excluded from the sample, notably, has comparable P/E ratio to Thailand by December 2017 (Weisblatt et al., 2018). In the same way, the Shenzhen stock exchange, which was also not included in the sample, has a P/E ratio that is about 1.4 times that of the Philippines stock exchange based on official data. These numbers suggest that expectations of corporate earnings per share in the region are relatively higher, which in turn make the stock markets more susceptible to further corrections when actual earnings fall short of expectations and cautious sentiment deepens even more.

In the currency sphere, the divergent nominal effective exchange rates of Emerging Asian economies persisted in the first six months of 2018 (Figure 1.26). The Chinese yuan has so far gained the most since the end of 2017, rising by 3.8% as of 25 June 2018, with the resurgence of foreign capital net placements and the persistent goods trade surplus, albeit the trend is declining since mid-May 2018. The Malaysian ringgit appreciated by about 2.6%, and the Thai baht by about 0.6% in the same period. Both Malaysia and Thailand continue to post robust financial account net liabilities and a healthy goods trade surplus (although this is narrowing in Thailand). By comparison, the Philippine peso lost about 5.6% of its value as the goods trade deficit widened further in January-May 2018, despite the modest growth in remittances from overseas workers. The Indonesian rupiah depreciated by 2.7%, and the Indian rupee by 3.9%. Downward pressure on the rupiah mainly came from portfolio investment outflows as well as dividend payments to foreign investors. A rising oil import bill has weighed down on the rupee, although income transfers tempered the decline. Against the US dollar, the ringgit has so far outperformed the currencies of regional peers through June 2018, whereas the rupee, the peso and the rupiah have been the weakest in the region.

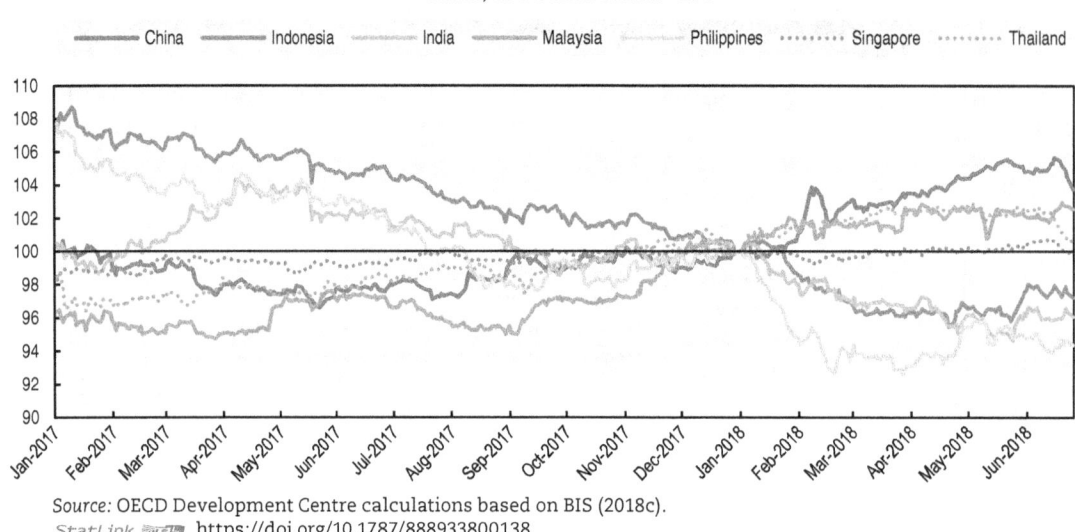

Figure 1.26. **Nominal effective exchange rate in Emerging Asia, 2017-18**
Index, 29 December 2017=100

Source: OECD Development Centre calculations based on BIS (2018c).
StatLink https://doi.org/10.1787/888933800138

Banking systems are generally sound as NPL-related pressures recede

Bank lending in Emerging Asia continues to grow healthily in 2018, although prevailing trends are mixed (Figure 1.27). Recent data reveal that bank credit extension has moderated in countries where lending growth rates have expanded in previous years (e.g. CLM countries, the Philippines and Viet Nam). On the other hand, in countries where the prior lending growth rates are comparably lower, the pace of bank credit extension has either gained a bit of traction (e.g. China, India, Malaysia, Singapore and Thailand) or increased at a steady pace (e.g. Indonesia). Brunei Darussalam is one exception, where bank lending is still tapering, although it is showing signs of mending; the economy, which just exited recession in 2017, is still trying to establish a good footing.

Return-on-equity (ROE) ratios of Emerging Asian banks mostly slid from 2016 to 2017, based on the latest data from the International Monetary Fund (IMF) *Financial Stability Indicators* database. The profitability of Myanmar's banks tumbled by more than half (from 9.7% in Q2 2016 to 3.5% in Q2 2017), while the ROE of banks in Cambodia, China, India, the Philippines and Thailand eased marginally based on the most recent data from a year earlier. On the other hand, Indonesian banks' ROE rose to 15.9% in 2017, the highest in the region, from 14.5% a year earlier. Banks in Brunei Darussalam, Malaysia and Singapore also saw their ROEs climb. Globally, the latest data in 2017 show that the ROEs of Emerging Asia's banking systems were conservative, compared with those outside the region. Only China, Indonesia and Singapore breached the 50th percentile in a sample covering 121 economies, and none reached the 75th percentile.

Total capital adequacy ratios (CAR) of banking sectors in Emerging Asia largely improved in 2017. The combined CAR of Indonesian banks reached 23.0% in 2017, which is 30 bps higher than the year earlier and tops the rates in China, India and ASEAN countries. Cambodian banks are in good stead, as well, with their combined CAR rising to 21.3% in Q3 2017, from 21.0% in Q3 2016. Thailand's banking sector similarly keeps ample capital per unit of risk weighted asset, with a CAR of 18.2% in 2016 and 2017. Brunei Darussalam's banking sector does the same, with a CAR of 18.1% in 2017, although it declined from the previous year. The banking sectors in Malaysia and Singapore are likewise not far off: they had identical CARs in 2016 and 2017, at 16.5% for Malaysia and 17.1% for Singapore.

Meanwhile, Myanmar's increased emphasis on banking stability pushed its banking sector's CAR up by 5.2 percentage points, to 16.0%, in Q2 2017, from just over 10.0% a year ago. Elsewhere in the region, the CAR of China's banking system nudged up to 13.2% in Q2 2017, from 13.1% in Q2 2016. The banking sectors in the Philippines and India, on the other hand, saw their CARs fall slightly in 2017, from a year before. The current level of capital adequacy in each country in the region is well above the requirement of the Basel 3 accord of 8.0% (total CAR) and 10.5% including the conservation buffer. However, international comparison reveals that the CAR of the banking systems of seven Emerging Asian economies (out of 10 with data in 2017) are below the 50th percentile in a sample of 122 economies, and only two (Indonesia and Cambodia) are above the 75th percentile.

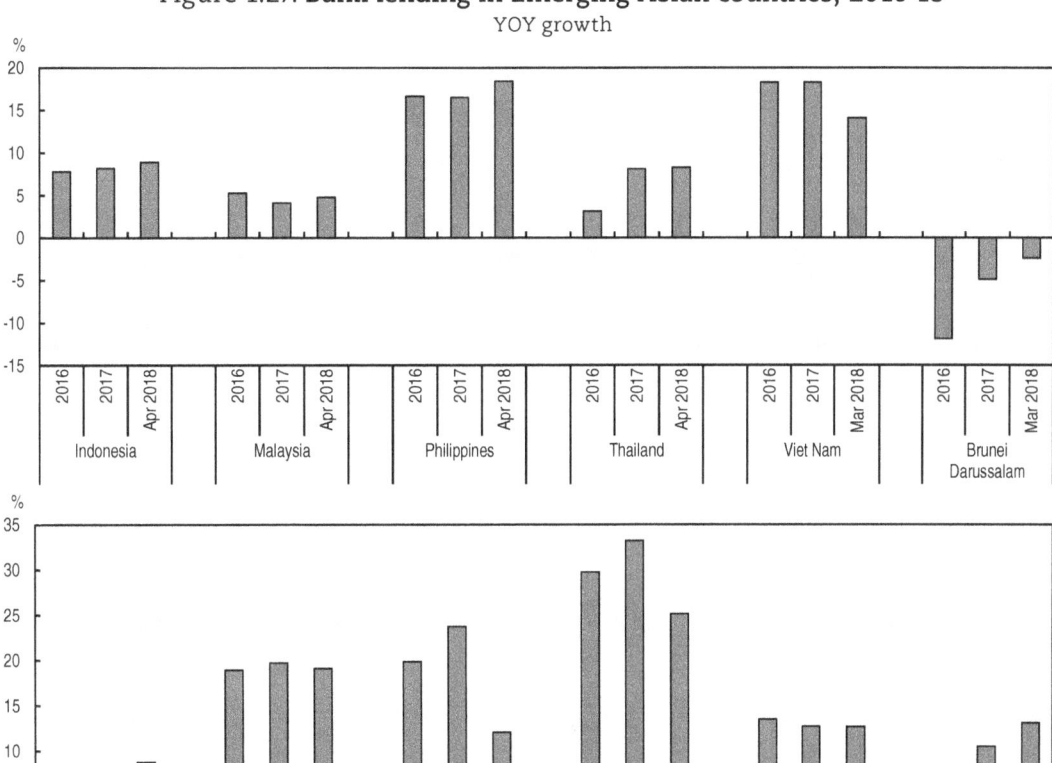

Figure 1.27. **Bank lending in Emerging Asian countries, 2016-18**
YOY growth

Note: Indonesia-Commercial and rural bank loans; Malaysia-Total banking sector loans; Philippines-Total banking sector loans; Thailand-Outstanding commercial bank credit; Viet Nam-Total outstanding bank credit; Brunei Darussalam-Commercial bank loans; Singapore-Loans and advances, ACU and DBU; Cambodia-Deposit money bank total gross loan; Lao PDR-Commercial bank total loans; Myanmar-Other depository corporation claims on private sector; China-Total loans; and India-Scheduled bank credit.
Source: OECD Development Centre calculations based on CEIC and national sources.
StatLink https://doi.org/10.1787/888933800157

NPL ratios have mainly gone down or stayed low in ASEAN-5 economies in the past 12 months (Figure 1.28). Bad debts in the books of the banks in Indonesia, Malaysia, the Philippines and Thailand have remained benign, aided by robust economic growth and vigilant monetary surveillance. However, in Viet Nam, NPLs are a prevailing policy issue. The NPL ratio based on banks' balance sheets slipped to 2.3% in 2017, from 2.6%

the previous year; this excludes the NPLs transferred to the Viet Nam Asset Management Company (VAMC). The VAMC bought an estimated VND 301 trillion of NPLs based on book value, or USD 13.2 billion, from 2013 to 2017, but it has resolved only about 20.0% of the acquisitions so far. Resolution 42, which became effective in August 2017, aimed to change the course of NPL disposal by improving the security of collaterals and opening the NPL market to foreign entities, which bodes well for the NPL trading volume in the secondary market.

Figure 1.28. **Non-performing loans ratio in Emerging Asian countries, 2017-18**

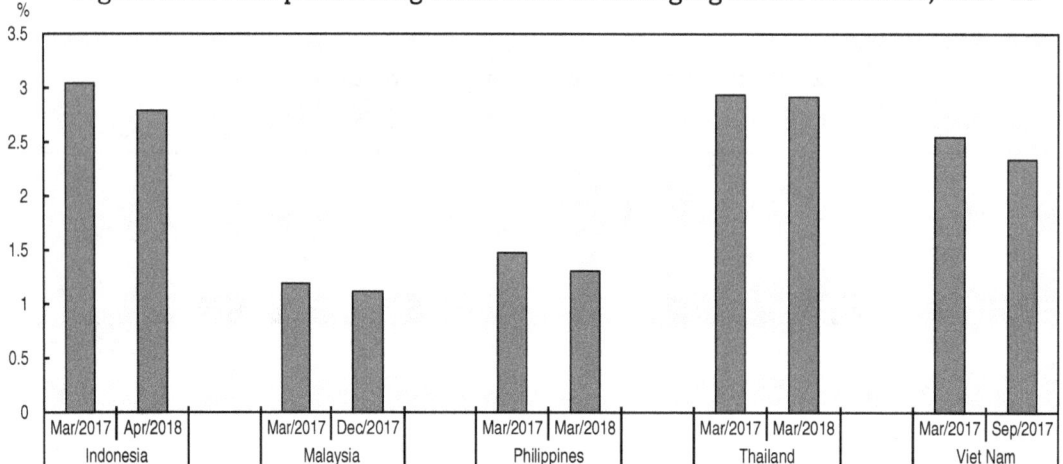

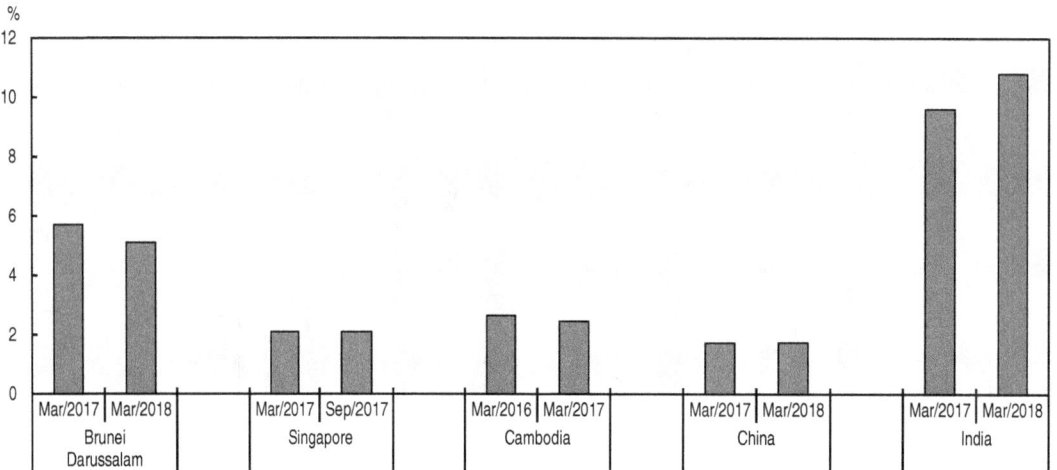

Note: Indonesia-Commercial banks; Malaysia-Total banking sector loans; Philippines-Universal and commercial banks; Thailand-Commercial banks; Viet Nam-Banking system; Brunei Darussalam-Commercial banks; Singapore-Banking system; Cambodia-Banking system; China-Commercial banks; and India-Scheduled commercial banks.
Source: OECD Development Centre calculations based on data from CEIC and national sources.
StatLink https://doi.org/10.1787/888933800176

NPL ratios in Brunei Darussalam and Singapore have decreased since 2016. The oil and gas sector's recovery contributed to the decline of NPL ratios in both countries. In CLM countries, banking sector stability was mixed. The NPL ratio of Cambodia's banking system was relatively modest – at 2.5% in March 2017, down from 2.7% in March 2016 – with economic activity matching credit expansion. In Lao PDR, the official NPL ratio in 2017 was about 3.0%. However, there remains outstanding issues pertaining to accounting and supervisory standards. In Myanmar, the banking system's NPL ratio is estimated at above 6.0%. Measures have been implemented in 2017 to strengthen financial stability and oversight; these include the conversion of overdrafts to term loans, the reduction in exposures deemed above prudential limits and tightened surveillance on lending to directors and related interests.

In China, the NPL ratio has been kept very low, at 1.74% in 2017 while the ratio of special mention loans declined, from 3.87% in 2016 to 3.49% in 2017. These trends are partly a result of the debt-equity swap programme, where bad loans are transferred to asset management companies established by banks. This way banks get hold of equity through their asset management arms. With some banks' liquidity positions generally improving, regulators changed the mandated loan loss provision to a range of 1.2% to 1.5% of impaired loans in February 2018, from a fixed 1.5% previously.

In India, banks' gross non-performing assets (GNPA) ratio climbed to 10.2% in September 2017, from 9.2% a year earlier. It is expected to climb to 11.1% (baseline scenario) in September 2018 (RBI, 2017). By end-September 2017, public banks saw their GNPA ratio rise to 13.5%, from 11.0% in the same period the previous year. Domestic private-sector banks' GNPA ratio also rose to 3.8%, from 3.6%, while foreign banks' ratio fell to 3.6%, from 4.1%. Among loan recipients, the industry sector has the highest GNPA ratio at 19.3%, up from 15.8% a year earlier. This increase was led by the industrial sub-sectors of basic metals and metal producers, engineering, mining and quarrying, and construction, which all have a GNPA ratio of more than 26.0%. The government allotted INR 800 billion, or USD 12.2 billion, to recapitalise public banks through bonds. The RBI also published a revised framework to resolve stressed assets in February 2018 in the hopes of quickly recognising bad debts (in cases of special mention or restructured loans) and expediting the resolution of these debts.

Fiscal consolidation sentiment mounts among governments in the region

Indonesia's national government budget deficit ratio (i.e. deficit relative to GDP) rose to 2.6% in 2017, from 2.5% a year earlier, though below the 2.9% target. Domestic revenue growth accelerated to 7.0% in 2017, from 3.4% in 2016, underpinned by the stronger tax growth due to improvement in global trade activity and the oil price recovery. Additionally, regulatory pullback in mineral ore exports increased non-tax revenues by more than 18.8%, from 2.5% in 2016. However, the revenue ratio (i.e. total revenue relative to GDP) fell for the fifth year since 2012, while the tax ratio (i.e. total tax relative to GDP) dropped to below 10.0%. Total expenditure ratio (total expenditure relative to GDP) also marginally decreased. For 2018, Indonesia aims to lower the budget deficit ratio to 2.2% on the premise that revenue and tax ratios will improve. Data in Q1 2018 peg the deficit-to-GDP ratio at 2.4% on an annualised four-quarter moving sum basis. Following the broader general government definition, the deficit ratio is estimated to be about 2.3% in 2018 and 2.2% in 2019 (Figure 1.29).

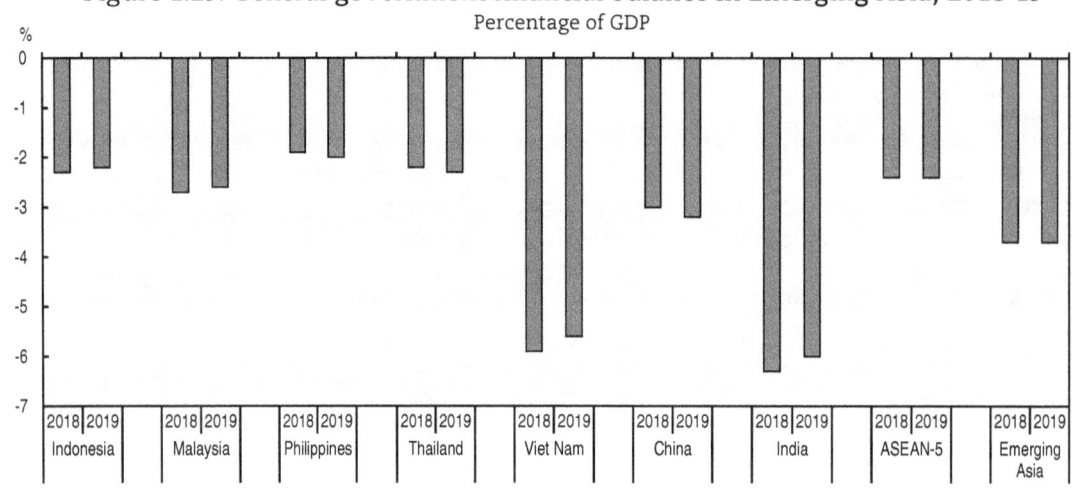

Figure 1.29. **General government financial balance in Emerging Asia, 2018-19**
Percentage of GDP

Note: The cut-off date for data used is 18 June 2018. The weighted averages are used for ASEAN average and Emerging Asia average. Data for India follow fiscal years. The projections of China, India and Indonesia are based on the OECD Economic Outlook No. 103 (database). General government balances data are not necessarily comparable to the budget balances published by national governments. Emerging Asia in this chart is comprised of ASEAN-5, China and India.
Source: OECD Development Centre, MPF-2018 (Medium-term Projection Framework).
StatLink ⟶ https://doi.org/10.1787/888933800195

Malaysia's budget deficit ratio declined to 3.0% in 2017 from 3.1% in 2016. Total revenues grew by 3.8% in 2017, after decreasing by 3.0% the previous year backed by acceleration in growth of corporate and individual income tax as well as petroleum income tax. Nonetheless, the revenue ratio slid to 16.3% in 2017, from 17.3% in 2016, whereas the tax ratio dropped to 13.1%, from 13.8%, over the same period. For 2018, the government aims to lower the deficit ratio to 2.8% (the target as of October 2017). Data in Q1 2018 indicate that the revenue ratio on an annualised basis has gone up marginally, to 16.6%, arresting the quarter-on-quarter decline for ten consecutive quarters while annualised budget deficit-to-GDP ratio of about 2.2%. Notably, the new government has abolished the GST tax effective June 2018, petrol and diesel subsidies have been reinstated while some bureaucratic lines are likely to be consolidated. Based on the broader general government framework, annual deficit ratio is projected to be about 2.7% in 2018 and 2.6% in 2019.

The budget deficit ratio of the Philippines decreased to 2.2% in 2017, from 2.4% in 2016. Total revenues in 2017 rose by 12.6%, propelled by the 13.6% growth in tax collection, the fastest rate since 2006. Consequently, revenue ratios rose by 15.6% in 2017, from 15.2% the previous year; tax ratios grew by 14.2%, from 13.7% in 2016. The expenditure ratio also moved up by about 30 bps. For 2018, the government targets a deficit ratio of 3.0%, even as it expects revenue and tax ratios to increase by about a percentage point after the passage of the first phase of the tax reform package in December 2017 (Box 1.5). As of Q1 2018, the annualised revenue ratio is about 15.9% whereas the annualised budget deficit ratio is estimated to be around 2.6%. In the context of general government, which is broader than national government, deficit ratio is estimated to settle at 1.9% in 2018 and 2.0% in 2019.

Thailand's annualised budget deficit ratio stood at 3.2% in the first six months of fiscal year 2018 (ending in September 2018), equalling the ratio in March 2017. Gross revenues rose by 2.6%, reversing the 1.9% decline in the same period in 2017, benefitting from larger contributions of revenue and customs departments. Yet, the annualised gross revenue ratio slid to 18.0% in March 2018, from 18.9% in March 2017 as do net revenue and tax ratios, which fell from 16.0% to 15.2% and from 15.7% to 15.1%, respectively over the same period. The total expenditure ratio also declined by roughly 60 bps. Thailand looks to incur a lower deficit ratio of about 2.8% in fiscal year 2018, from 3.5% in fiscal year 2017. An e-commerce value-added tax (VAT) is currently in the offing to increase revenue inflows, following the new excise tax law which became effective in September 2017. Nonetheless, the government also implemented a tourism tax-rebate policy, a corporate income-tax reduction related to the newly mandated minimum wage, and corporate and personal income tax cuts related to child care. On a broader general government basis, the annual deficit ratio is projected to be about 2.2% in 2018 and 2.3% in 2019.

The budget deficit ratio of Viet Nam has risen to 6.7% in 2017, from 5.6% in 2016, though the primary deficit decreased to 3.5%, from 4.2%, over the same period. Revenues grew by 17.0% in 2017, up from 10.5% in 2016, largely due to substantial improvements in income tax and VAT payments. However, spending ratio also rose largely accounted for by development investment and debt principal payments. For 2018, the government expects the primary deficit ratio to inch up to 3.7%, and the overall deficit to be about 6.6% (based on the VND 363.28 trillion borrowing plan). The government is deliberating revenue measures to further boost collection in the medium term; these measures concern the VAT, the number of income brackets, and additional levies on sugary drinks, cigarettes and vehicles, among others. With this backdrop and based on the broader framework of general government, annual deficit-to-GDP ratio is projected to be about 5.9% in 2018 and 5.6% in 2019.

Brunei Darussalam's budget deficit is estimated to have narrowed to about 10% in fiscal year 2017 (ending March 2018) from over 16% in the previous year. While revenues are estimated to have risen by more than 10.0% in 2017, the expenditure level was pared by about 5.3%. In 2018, the government projects a rise in revenues of about 9.0% and the budget deficit to decrease by another 16.0%, given the prevailing proposal to keep the spending target unchanged.

Singapore's budget surplus rose to 2.1% of GDP in fiscal year 2017 (ending March 2018), from 1.4% in the previous year. The revenue ratio inclusive of net investment income has inched up to 19.6% in 2017, from 19.3% in 2016, on the strength of improvement in collections off corporate income tax, customs and excise duties, duty stamps and statutory board's contribution. Total spending ratio (including transfers) declined by 30 bps during the period. The government anticipates a negative balance in 2018, although this will be relatively small, at 0.1% of GDP. Operating revenues are projected to fall on lower contributions from statutory boards, duty stamps and vehicle-quota collections. Spending is expected to increase sharply when large rail projects get under way, although some of these projects are contingent on the outcome of negotiations with Malaysia's new government.

Following a surplus year, Cambodia ended 2017 with a deficit estimated to be 0.7% of GDP, or 0.9%, incorporating expenditure adjustments. Total revenues improved to 18.6% in 2017, from 17.5% in 2016, while tax revenues improved to 16.0% in 2017, from 15.0% the previous year. In the same way, the spending ratio went up markedly in 2017 to make up for the contraction in the previous year. The continuous improvement in fiscal ratios since hitting trough in 2009 can be attributed to the adoption of the Revenue Mobilisation Strategy and the Public Financial Reform Management Programme. Data by the end of April 2018 show that revenues rose by about 1.6% YOY, while spending grew by 9.6%.

Lao PDR's budget deficit ratio came in at 5.5% in 2017, from 5.2% in 2016. The revenue ratio (including grants) slid to 16.1% in 2017, down from 16.3% in 2016, despite increase in level of about 5.4%. The notable improvement in VAT collection and auxiliary taxes pushed tax revenues to grow 3.3% from 0.4% the year prior. But, as a proportion of GDP, tax ratio also declined to about 12.0% from 12.7%. In contrast, the spending ratio rose slightly in 2017 on the account of capital expenditures which increased by 64.4% in 2017, following the 37.8% reduction in 2016. In 2018, the government looks to incur a lower budget deficit ratio of 5.4%, which though lower than in 2017, is still high relative to the medium-term deficit ratio target of 4.0%.

Myanmar's state budget deficit ratio is estimated to have risen to 5.1% in fiscal year 2017 (ending March 2018), from about 4.1% in the previous year, on larger outlays to infrastructure, education and health, after substantially undershooting its spending target in 2016. With the government's decision to move its fiscal year, a separate fiscal program covering the interim six-month period (April 2018 to September 2018) had been introduced. During the period, the government committed to refrain from requesting supplemental budgets and pushed funding decisions on new projects to the new fiscal year which will run from October 2018 to September 2019. Nonetheless, funding requirements of ongoing projects are seen to push the deficit ratio to 5.0%. Meanwhile, the 2018 Union Tax Law lowered the special goods tax on vehicles to 10.0%, from 20.0%, and enumerated a new list of goods and services exempted from commercial tax. To support business, the government removed all forms of withholding taxes on goods, services, leases and royalties.

China's headline budget deficit ratio was 3.7% in 2017, slightly down from 3.8% in 2016. Total revenues increased by 8.2%, outpacing the 4.8% growth in 2016. This growth in total revenues was buttressed by tax revenues, which grew by 10.7% in 2017, or more than double the 4.4% increase in 2016, while non-tax revenues contracted by 3.5%, after rising by 6.9% in the previous year. The stronger tax performance during the year stemmed largely from improvements in VAT collection as well as the phasing out of a number of user charges in an attempt to reduce burden. Expenditure growth was equally robust at 8.3%, up from 6.8% in the previous year, due to stepped up spending on some priority items such as the environment and health. The government raised the possibility of lowering VAT applied on manufacturing and transportation enterprises; reforming personal income taxation; extending the scope of preferential tax policy covering SMEs, logistics companies, venture capital and angel investment; and standardising various industry charges. Based on a broader general government framework, the deficit ratio is forecast to be about 3.0% in 2018 and 3.2% in 2019.

India's budget deficit ratio steadied at 3.5% in fiscal year 2017 (ending March 2018), unchanged from 2016. Gross receipts grew by 7.6% in 2017, more slowly than the previous year's 14.6%. Incorporating transfers and surcharges, revenues ratio settled at about 13.3% in 2017, moderately lower than the 13.5% in 2016, while the gross tax ratio improved to 11.4%, from 11.2% over the same period. The robust growth in payments of corporate and income tax as well as non-debt capital receipts were offset by the contraction in customs, excise and service taxes. Non-tax revenues also dipped by about a third in 2017 following a modest gain in 2016. In 2018, the deficit ratio is estimated to settle at 3.3%. The government counts on the new goods and services tax, implemented in 2017, to bolster collections. On a general government basis, the deficit ratio is projected to come in at 6.3% in 2018 and 6.0% in 2019.

> **Box 1.5. Recent tax reforms in some Emerging Asian countries**
>
> Tax revenue in relation to GDP is still low in Emerging Asian countries, compared with OECD countries. In 2015, for instance, total tax revenue was 11.8% of GDP in Indonesia and 17% in the Philippines, while it was 34.3% in OECD countries (OECD, 2017b). Emerging Asian countries, therefore, have a large potential to improve tax revenue. Some countries in the region recently implemented major tax reforms to address this issue.
>
> Indonesia has introduced a series of tax reforms since the 2000s to improve revenue collection and the efficiency of tax administration (Figure 1.30). The tax amnesty programme, launched in 2016, ended in March 2017 with a total of IDR 4 866 trillion (Indonesian rupiahs) in declared assets and IDR 147 trillion repatriated. The government is continuing its comprehensive tax reforms and, in late 2016, created a tax reform team to support this agenda. The series of reforms, planned to be completed in 2020, focuses on five pillars: improving regulations and strengthening human resources, organisation,

Box 1.5. **Recent tax reforms in some Emerging Asian countries** *(cont.)*

databases, the information-technology (IT) system and business process. Improving the IT system is especially crucial to support the OECD Automatic Exchange of Information (AEOI) initiative, which will start this year. Tax reform is also part of the efforts to boost investment. In March 2018, a new regulation on tax holidays was put in place. Corporate taxpayers investing in pioneer industries, covering 17 sectors, can apply for these new incentives. In addition, the government issued new tax regulations to accelerate the process of restitution, simplify the procedure of exemption from value-added tax (VAT) and sales tax on luxury goods for international agencies, and simplify the audits of upstream oil and gas activities; these audits will be carried out jointly by the Directorate General of Tax of the Ministry of Finance, the Upstream Oil and Gas Regulatory Special Task Force (SKK Migas) and the Financial and Development Supervisory Board (BPKP). The government targeted IDR 1 618 trillion in tax revenue in 2018.

Figure 1.30. **Tax reform packages in Indonesia**

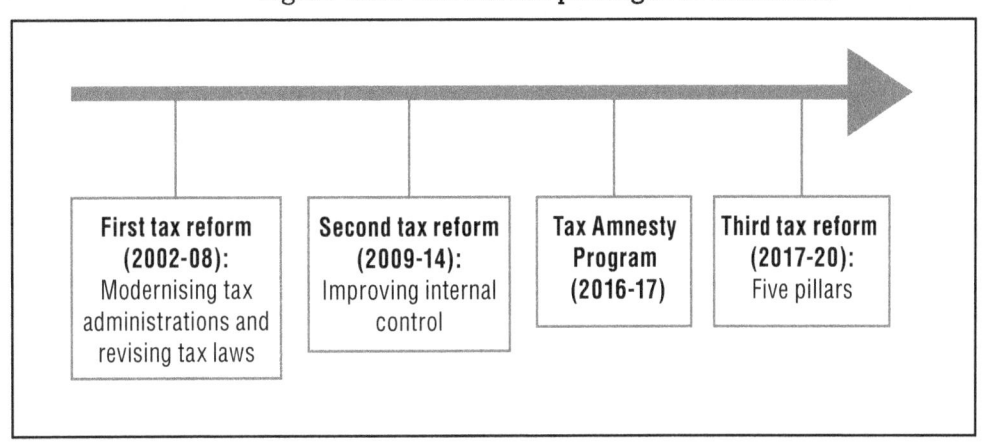

Source: Ministry of Finance, Indonesia.

The Philippines recently started a comprehensive tax-reform package to enhance the tax system and bolster revenue collection. The first package of the reform, called Tax Reform for Acceleration and Inclusion (TRAIN) 1A, passed into law in December 2017. This measure is expected to take in an estimated PHP 89.9 billion (Philippine pesos) in revenues, or about 0.5% of GDP, in 2018 and PHP 786.4 billion, or about 0.74% of GDP, through 2022. Seventy per cent of the proceeds are earmarked for infrastructure (Build Build Build projects), military installations, sports and education facilities, and potable drinking water in public spaces, while 30% will be spent on education, health, nutrition and hunger-alleviation programmes, social protection, employment, housing and sugarcane-industry development. The law has introduced notable changes in the tax regime (Table 1.3). The second reform package, called TRAIN 1B, was submitted to Congress in January 2018; the Department of Finance initially hoped it would be approved in March 2018. The measure is expected to yield revenues of PHP 38.9 billion in 2018 and PHP 182.7 billion through 2022, although the delay in legislative approval could narrow the potential intake for this time frame.

> **Box 1.5. Recent tax reforms in some Emerging Asian countries** *(cont.)*
>
> **Table 1.3. Main features of TRAIN 1A**
>
> | Tax rate and coverage reductions or simplifications | Tax rate increases and coverage expansion |
> | --- | --- |
> | • Lowered personal income-tax rates, reduced the number of income brackets and raised the tax exemption cap on the mandatory 13th-month pay.
• Imposed a flat rate of 6% for estate and donor's taxes, from a variable rate that could go up to 15% for estate tax and 20% for donor tax.
• Raised the VAT exemption threshold of businesses from PHP 1.9 million in gross sales to PHP 3 million.
• Granted VAT exemption to drugs and medicines for diabetes, high cholesterol and hypertension (starting 2019), and socialised and mass housing projects (starting 2021).
• Raised the ceiling of the value of family homes exempted from estate tax from PHP 1 million to PHP 10 million. | • Raised taxes/excise tax rates levied on cars, fuel, tobacco, coal, cosmetic surgery, tobacco and selected sweetened beverages.
• Raised the documentary stamp tax and the tax rates for untraded stocks, stock transactions and foreign currency deposit units.
• Streamlined VAT-exempt items by repealing 54 of 61 special laws deemed non-essential. |
>
> *Source:* DOF (2018a; 2018b).
>
> Malaysia also carried out tax reform, mainly to reduce the country's rising cost of living. The new government fulfilled a campaign promise to abolish the Goods and Services Tax (GST) in its first 100 days of office, and it reduced the GST from 6% to zero, starting from 1 June 2018 (see Box 1.1).

Challenges for robust growth

Overall, Emerging Asia – Southeast Asia, China and India – is projected to experience favourable growth over the near term. However, maintaining robust growth requires careful attention to several challenges:

- the impact of rising interest rates in advanced economies, in particular the United States, on Emerging Asian economies;
- the implementation of planned infrastructure projects; and
- the acceleration of regional integration amidst rising protectionism.

Rising interest rates in advanced economies are a risk for Emerging Asian economies

The ongoing rise in the cost of money globally, owing to monetary normalisation in advanced economies remains a notable risk to Emerging Asia's economic growth. The upward movement in US interest rate together with the sharp uptick in global oil prices, which have partly instigated a build-up in inflation pressures and the stress on domestic currencies, have already prompted a number of central banks in Emerging Asia to raise their policy rates (Table 1.4). Notably, the rate hike cycle is still at an early stage in the US and has not even commenced in Europe and Japan, notwithstanding the looming reduction in the balance sheets of major central banks and the planned fiscal expansion in some large economies.

Table 1.4. **Summary of recent central bank policy-rate changes in Emerging Asia**

Country	Policy rate action	Primary underlying reasons
India	6 June 2018: RBI raised the policy repo rate, reverse repo rate, marginal standing facility rate and the bank rate by 25 bps each.	RBI raised rates to achieve the medium-term target of 4.0% (+/2 percentage points) for consumer price index (CPI) inflation, which has responded strongly to the recent global oil price volatility.
Indonesia	17 May 2018: BI raised the seven-day reverse repo rate, deposit facility rate and lending facility rates by 25 bps each.	BI increased rates to maintain economic stability amid escalating global financial market risks and the global liquidity downturn. BI will continue with rupiah exchange-rate stabilisation measures, while maintaining adequate liquidity in the foreign exchange and money markets.
	30 May 2018: BI raised the seven-day reverse repo rate, deposit facility rate and lending facility rates by 25 bps each.	The rate hikes were a pre-emptive move to maintain exchange rate stability against a higher-than-expected US Federal Funds Rate increase and rising risks in the global financial market, while keeping inflation in check. BI will continue to intervene in the foreign-exchange and government-securities markets to stabilise rupiah exchange rates, adjust fair prices in the financial markets, and maintain adequate liquidity in the money and interbank swap markets.
	29 June 2018: BI raised the 7-day Reverse Repo rate, deposit facility rate and lending facility rates by 50 bps each.	The rate hikes were a pre-emptive measure to maintain the domestic financial market's competitiveness against several countries' changing monetary policies as well as high global uncertainty consistent with the framework of dual intervention policy in the foreign exchange market and government securities markets.
Malaysia	25 January 2018: BNM raised the overnight policy rate and its corresponding floor and ceiling rates by 25 bps.	BNM increased rates to normalise the degree of monetary accommodation, given the economy's reassuring strength, and to prevent the build-up of risks that could arise from protracted low interest rates.
Philippines	10 May 2018: BSP raised the overnight reverse repurchase rate, overnight lending rate and overnight deposit rate by 25 bps each.	BSP raised rates to arrest an increase in inflation expectations amid broadening inflation pressures. BSP noted that it continues to survey the domestic and global economic environment, including the potential impact of the monetary policy normalisation in advanced economies.
	20 June 2018: BSP raised overnight reverse repurchase rate, overnight lending rate and overnight deposit rate by 25 bps each.	BSP raised rates to mitigate upside risks to inflation outlook and the risk of second-round effects. BSP will remain vigilant against domestic and international developments, including excessive peso volatility, that could affect the outlook for inflation.

Source: OECD Development Centre compilation based on national central bank sources.

The risk of monetary normalisation in advanced economies will affect Emerging Asia's economies largely through capital flows and domestic demand channels, if it proceeds faster than anticipated or if it prolongs and accompanied by other external risk factors. The capital flow channel concerns outflows including the effects working through exchange-rate. The domestic demand channel, on the other hand, concerns the potential impact on private consumption, public spending and investment – and by extension, financial market stability in the context of asset-side squeeze (i.e. mainly the decline in asset prices and an increased difficulty in recovering loans). The extent of the potential impact depends on an array of domestic factors. Monetary policy normalisation can spill over through the trade channel as well.

Changes in US monetary policy will affect capital flows in Emerging Asia

According to Anaya, Hachula and Offermanns (2017), the US Fed's unconventional monetary policy is associated with increased capital inflows to emerging market economies. In turn, the increase in inflows is accompanied by a higher growth in real output, a rise in equity returns, an appreciation of the real exchange rate and a decline in the real lending rate. These findings are in part shared by Punzi and Chantapacdepong (2017). It remains to be seen how extensive the reversal will be once the normalisation process takes hold, considering the unprecedented scale of major economies' quantitative easing. The impact is expected to vary by country, depending on their macro fundamentals.

The withdrawals that can be associated with the changes in US interest rate are limited thus far, based on available data. The domestic growth prospect is one factor. The realisation of the repeated assurances of central bank authorities in the US, Europe and Japan to avoid surprises concerning the pace of monetary policy changes has also given the capital markets in Emerging Asia the elbow room to correct relatively smoothly. Yields of benchmark European debt papers have stayed comparatively low and have been moving sideways for a time; this has limited investors' alternatives, placing emerging markets with strong fundamentals under a favourable light among institutional investors. Finally, the relatively healthy expectations of the region's domestic corporate earnings partly helped ease the stress.

The threat of net capital outflow in the near-term arguably remains benign at this point as well. The benchmark bond yield differentials, which have narrowed substantially since 2013, appear to be widening (refer to Figure 1.22). Incidentally, the correlation between the ten-year benchmark bond yields of most Emerging Asian countries and the United States seems to have strengthened since the end of 2017 (Table 1.5), except for China and Viet Nam. However, the conditions can change in a short period. The build-up in vulnerabilities, which can potentially cause foreign capital pull back, needs careful attention. For instance, faster local inflation can drag down real returns on investment. Market volatility, which had been muted for a time, has returned strongly in 2018. Credit default swap spreads, which are indicative of credit risk perception, are also gradually going up again. These could be signals of the degree of market apprehensions that can result in flight to safety when market disruptions happen. Moreover, markets are gearing up more intently for larger public spending in advanced economies, particularly the United States, at a time when global liquidity is expected to moderate going forward.

Table 1.5. **Correlation of Emerging Asia benchmarket bond yields with US benchmark bond yields**

1-year yields, 10-day moving average

	Before the US started the rate hikes		After the US started the rate hikes		Between 16 December 2015 and end-2016		Between end-2016 and end-2017		Since end-2017	
China	-0,5757	**	0,7841	**	0,3968	**	0,9185	**	-0,9829	**
India	-0,6353	**	-0,3565	**	-0,6451	**	0,1192		0,5538	**
Indonesia	0,2857	**	-0,7390	**	0,0438		-0,9171	**	0,7895	**
Malaysia	0,4046		0,7741		-0,2775		0,7387		0,8809	
Philippines	0,3881	**	0,8800	**	0,0483		0,7865	**	0,9642	**
Singapore	0,7930	**	0,9242	**	0,0479		0,8738	**	0,6864	**
Thailand	-0,4669	**	-0,2900	**	0,6292	**	-0,8255	**	0,6046	**
Viet Nam	-0,1666	**	-0,8187	**	-0,3049	**	-0,3048	**	-0,8921	**
Sample size	1033		641		272		260		109	

Notes: Sample comprises all weekdays from 2 January 2012 to 31 May 2018. For non-trading weekdays, yields during the preceding trading weekday are used. The US Fed started hiking its policy rate on 16 December 2015. *Coefficient color spectrum (-1 to 1):*
* = significant at 5.0%, ** = significant at 1.0%
Source: OECD Development Centre calculations based on data from Fusion Media Ltd. (2018), www.investing.com.

Interest rate hikes in advanced economies may dampen domestic demand in the region

The prevailing upward trend in interest rates may change the course of domestic spending in Emerging Asia. US monetary policy – both before and after the period of quantitative easing – has spilled over to Asia through yields and credit growth (Miyajima, Mohanty and Yetman, 2014). The United States' low term premium, for instance, was associated with low domestic yields and rapid bank credit expansion in Asia. According to Chen et al. (2015), the spillover effects across countries vary in terms of their impact on credit, inflation and output; furthermore, cross-border monetary policy spillovers from the United States can determine real sector and financial market instability. The responsiveness of domestic central banks and national governments is crucial in dealing with externally induced weakness in domestic demand. Amid a sustained climb in interest rates, national authorities must mitigate domestically grown risks that can spook investor confidence, such as delays in large-scale projects and drastic regulatory changes that could dampen the business climate. Even if US monetary policy adjusts upwards moderately faster than the current pace, its impact on the real economy of the ASEAN-5 countries (Indonesia, Malaysia, the Philippines, Thailand and Viet Nam) will be small, so long as economic fundamentals hold up (OECD, 2016).

Household debt could weigh on private consumption. As loan payments rise, the share of income spent on goods and services is reduced. Notably, as reported by Punzi (2018), household debt rose markedly in Malaysia, Thailand and Viet Nam from 2009 to 2016, prompting monetary authorities to take measures to slow down the pace of debt accumulation. Consumption in dollarised economies is also susceptible to currency-related shocks.

Empirical studies support the conjecture of a negative relationship between interest rates and consumption, although with relevant caveats. For instance, Kapoor and Ravi (2009) posited that this customary view on the link between interest rates and consumption seems to hold in India, but noted that "consumers do not perfectly smooth consumption across expected interest rate changes" and that the impact is weaker in the long term than in the short. Aizenman, Cheung, and Ito (2017), who examined the link among interest rates, private savings and consumption in various countries, argued that the final effect of interest rates on private savings and consumption depends on the levels of interest rates (i.e. breaching certain thresholds can change the magnitude of the effect). However, the study highlighted that in countries where output volatility, financial market development and dependency are absent, the negative relationship is not robust and even reverses.

Monetary policy normalisation can spill over through the trade channel, as well. Borodin and Strokov (2011) argue that relative interest-rate levels affect the structure of exports or product specialisation. Another line of thinking is that higher capital costs globally can weaken domestic aggregate demand and therefore dampen trade. Moreover, the impact on countries will likely depend on relative movements in exchange rates and commodity prices, which also spring from interest-rate changes. Furthermore, rising US interest rates had been accompanied by the strengthening of the US dollar, the currency in which most internationally traded goods are priced. The DXY index, which tracks the value of the US dollar against the currencies of the United States' major trade partners, has risen steeply since mid-2014, oscillated around a flat trend since then, though the bias had been on the upside since the beginning of 2018. A strong US dollar tends to increase imported inflation in many countries.

Given these risks, Emerging Asian countries should pro-actively monitor the health of their banks and financial markets in general, so as to contain potential additional sources of investor apprehension. Economies with large stocks of bad loans must continue trying to gradually work out these listings in the balance sheets of financial institutions. A key challenge is to strike a good balance in monetary policymaking between keeping domestic demand buoyant, on the one hand, and responding to exchange-rate movements and the prices of global commodities such as oil, on the other. Economies that rely heavily on the US dollar for domestic transactions have additional reason to be cautious and to develop their monetary policy toolkits, possibly in co-ordination with multilateral agencies and more developed central banks in the region. Fiscal prudence is vital, as well. Optimising public spending, particularly on big-ticket projects, can mean substantial savings over time, given the increasing cost of financing.

Infrastructure investments may boost growth prospects, if implementation challenges can be addressed

The planned investments in developing, upgrading and maintaining infrastructure in Emerging Asia present ambiguous risks for the region's economic outlook over the near and medium term. During construction, infrastructure projects can crowd out other investments, but they also provide economic stimulus. This stimulus can be substantial, and the multiplier effect of public investment is the highest in countries where the public capital stock is the lowest, where the stimulus is combined with complementary actions in other space need policy areas and when countries act collectively (Mourougane et al., 2016). Operational infrastructure can increase efficiency and demand, as well as induce economic activity (Oosterhaven and Knaap, 2003). These longer-term benefits are particularly important to Emerging Asian economies, most of which need more high-quality infrastructure. However, investment levels may not be sufficient to meet rising demand. In addition, and more relevantly for near-term growth prospects, difficulties in efficiently implementing infrastructure projects mean that the planned investments' potential gains may not be realised.

Significant investment is planned for the near future to address Emerging Asia's infrastructure gaps

Insufficient infrastructure significantly constrains economic development in Emerging Asia. Although Singapore is ranked second globally in terms of overall infrastructure quality, according to the World Economic Forum, infrastructure quality is judged to be particularly low in Thailand (ranked 67th globally), Indonesia (68th), Lao PDR (83rd), Viet Nam (89th), Cambodia (99th) and the Philippines (133rd) (WEF, 2017).[4]

Across most of Emerging Asia, the levels of infrastructure investment fall below needed levels (Figure 1.31). The gap between estimated infrastructure investment levels and needs is the greatest in the lower-income Emerging Asian economies; in Cambodia, investment was estimated to total 8.2% of GDP in 2017, below the needed 11.6%. Compared with needs, investment is also relatively low in Myanmar and Viet Nam, which, along with Cambodia, have the greatest needs for infrastructure investment relative to GDP. In high-income Singapore, on the other hand, estimated infrastructure investment and needs are the lowest as a share of GDP, with no investment gap. While the amount of infrastructure investment in Emerging Asian countries is generally insufficient, the allocations of the shares of this investment are closely aligned with estimated need by sector. Energy infrastructure has attracted the most investment in several Emerging Asian countries – Malaysia, the Philippines, Singapore, Thailand, Viet Nam and India – where the need for investment in energy infrastructure is also the greatest. Road transport infrastructure is another relatively important area; it accounts for the largest share of infrastructure investment in Indonesia and China. Telecommunications infrastructure attracts the most investment in Cambodia and Myanmar.

Figure 1.31. **Estimated infrastructure investment and needs in Emerging Asian countries, 2017**

Percentage of GDP

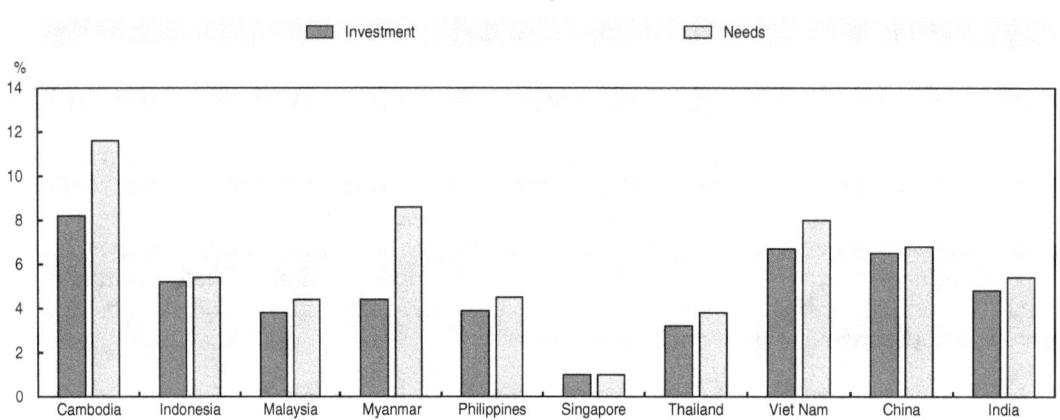

Note: Estimates of infrastructure investment and need are not available for Brunei Darussalam or Lao PDR.
Source: Global Infrastructure Hub (2018), *Infrastructure Outlook* (database), https://outlook.gihub.org.
StatLink https://doi.org/10.1787/888933800214

Recent announcements show that the region's governments are committed to improving infrastructure. The draft budget announced by Indonesia's government in August 2017 allocated IDR 409 trillion (Indonesian rupiahs) to road, rail and other projects, up from IDR 387.3 trillion in the previous year. Malaysia's 2018 budget allocated MYR 210 billion (Malaysian ringgits) for infrastructure projects, with a majority of this funding dedicated to rail and public transport projects, including the East Coast Rail Link, the Kuala Lumpur-Singapore High Speed Rail and the third phase of the mass rapid transit system project. In the Philippines, about PHP 1 trillion (Philippines pesos) of the budget is dedicated to infrastructure, which is to be funded in part through tax reforms. In addition, about PHP 20 billion has been allocated over two years for the reconstruction of Marawi. In the 2018 Thai budget, the capital expenditure appropriation is THB 659.9 billion (Thai baht), or 22.8% of the total. In addition to 51 ongoing projects, the Ministry of Transport plans eight new projects for 2018, with a total budget of THB 100 billion. THB 1.5 trillion was committed over five years to infrastructure development in the Eastern Economic Corridor (EEC). In Viet Nam, VND 150 trillion (Vietnamese dong) has been allocated for infrastructure development over 2016-20. Key ongoing projects in the country include the construction of a 1 800-kilometre expressway from Ha Noi to Ho Chi Minh City.

Brunei Darussalam's 2018 budget includes allocations for improving information technology infrastructure in government, public transport, public parks and other projects. Singapore's budget outlines an increase in infrastructure spending, with work ongoing on major projects, including the high-speed rail link with Kuala Lumpur, a new airport terminal at Changi Airport and a new mega-port. Cambodia's government announced plans in August 2017 for USD 5.4 billion (United States dollars) in public investment over the following three years, to fund the implementation of 586 development projects, with about a quarter of the funding to be dedicated to infrastructure. The Lao PDR government issued a 15-year USD 420 million bond on the Thai debt market in October 2017; the bond will be used to pay off outstanding debt and to fund infrastructure investments. According to China's Ministry of Transport, transport infrastructure spending in the country in 2018 will be similar to that of 2017, for which CNY 2.6 trillion (Chinese Yuan renminbi) in spending was targeted at the beginning of the year. India's budget included plans to increase infrastructure investment, particularly in roads and railways, as the government also plans infrastructure upgrades over the next five years.

In many respects, the region is doing well in implementing its infrastructure projects. Among the ASEAN-5 economies (Indonesia, Malaysia, the Philippines, Thailand and Viet Nam), quarterly YOY growth in added value in the construction sector exceeded that of GDP in most of 2017, except in Thailand, where growth in construction fell behind that of the broader economy (a change from the previous two years, in which the construction sector grew at a faster rate). Nevertheless, Thailand reported a 47.0% YOY increase in state-owned enterprises' (SOEs) disbursement of investment budgets from October 2017 to January 2018, due to work on large-scale projects, including the construction of new lines by the Mass Rapid Transit Authority of Thailand (MRTA). According to a report by the Philippines' Department of Budget and Management, an increase in disbursements on infrastructure and other capital outlays in the country in 2017 was due to projects carried out by the Department of Public Works and Highways, the Department of National Defense, the Department of the Interior and Local Government-Philippine National Police, the Department of Education and others. More generally, recent actual capital expenditure has been close to budget appropriations or estimates in many countries in the region (Table 1.6).

Table 1.6. **Recent capital expenditure in selected Emerging Asian countries**

Country	Time period	Budget appropriation or expected expenditure	Actual expenditure
Lao PDR	FY 2014/15	LAK 10.7 trillion	LAK 11. 4 trillion
Philippines	FY 2017	PHP 773.3 billion	PHP 858.1 billion
Singapore	FY 2017	SGD 18.8 billion	SGD 17.8 billion
Thailand	FY 2017	THB 632.6 billion	THB 380.8 billion
India	2016/17	INR 3.1 trillion	INR 2.8 trillion

Note: Singapore totals refer to "development expenditure", which includes "expenses that represent a longer-term investment or result in the formation of a capitalisable asset".
Source: OECD Development Centre compilation, based on national sources.

Upcoming regional events are likely to increase countries' motivation to implement and complete infrastructure projects. Several elections are expected in the near term. Public investment in democracies tends to peak 21 to 25 months before elections, including through the construction of high-visibility projects ready to be built (Gupta, Liu and Mulas-Garanados, 2015). Planned upcoming general elections in Cambodia in July 2018, in Thailand in November 2018, in Indonesia in April 2019, and in India in April or May 2019; a midterm election in the Philippines in May 2019; and regional elections in Indonesia in June 2018 are likely to provide additional incentives to announce and deliver on infrastructure projects. The 2018 Asian Games, to be held in August and September 2018 in Indonesia, also provide a strong motivation for the completion of associated development projects. Indonesia's government had set aside IDR 30 trillion for these projects, including ongoing light-rail construction projects in co-host cities Jakarta and Palembang.

New approaches may help to facilitate the implementation of planned infrastructure projects

Successful infrastructure projects are those that are completed on time, within their allocated budget and at the expected level of quality, but risks are present in the form of delays and other complications arising from various factors. Delays in completing infrastructure projects tend to be more common in developing countries. However, some factors contributing to delays in advanced economies may also be relevant elsewhere; these include reduced funding, communication failures, delayed disbursements, issues regarding contractors' site management, and legislative or regulatory barriers (Okeyo, Rambo and Odundo, 2015; Sambasivan and Soon, 2007). Factors such as these have complicated infrastructure implementation in Emerging Asia. For example, the Asian Development Bank (ADB) estimates that only 36.0% of the sovereign projects reviewed in 2015-17, which include many infrastructure projects, were finished on time, and that delayed projects were finished with a 2.8-year lag (ADB, 2017a). In Emerging Asia, many projects approved in the past five years have not been completed. Among ASEAN members, 219 ADB sovereign projects (74.0% of the total) approved from 2013 to 2017 remain at the approval or active stage (Table 1.7). Across Emerging Asia, 433 projects (70.4% of the total) are not yet closed.

Difficulties in co-ordinating with international and private sector partners delayed several major infrastructure projects recently. Talks began in 2014 for a USD 5.2 billion high-speed rail project between Thailand and China, but prolonged negotiations between the Thai government and Chinese contractors delayed the start of construction to December 2017. The project for the Hanthawaddy International Airport – a new airport in Bago Region, Myanmar – was started in 2001, though the framework agreement with a consortium of contractors from Singapore and Japan was signed in January 2016, with the first phase estimated to cost USD 1.5 billion. However, disputes on costs led to the agreement expiring in January 2018 without being renewed. Concerns about public debt have impeded progress on Official Development Assistance (ODA)-backed infrastructure projects in Viet Nam, including the development of the metro line in Ho Chi Minh City.

Uncertainties regarding the financing of infrastructure projects in Indonesia led to a drop in the value of construction stocks in 2017, even as the Jakarta Composite Index experienced strong growth.

Table 1.7. **Status of ADB sovereign projects in Emerging Asia, 2013-17**

	Number of projects		
	Approved only	Active	Closed
Cambodia	3	31	11
Indonesia	2	37	14
Lao PDR	1	22	7
Malaysia	0	0	1
Myanmar	0	35	10
Philippines	2	24	17
Thailand	1	3	3
Viet Nam	5	53	14
China	8	115	83
India	12	79	22
ASEAN total	14	205	77
Emerging Asia total	34	399	182

Notes: Status as of 7 February 2018. "Active" projects are those that have been approved and have met the conditions for effectiveness for at least one source of finance, and is ready for or already being implemented. No projects were listed for this period for Brunei Darussalam or Singapore.
Source: ADB (2108b), *ADB Sovereign Projects* (database), https://data.adb.org/dataset/adb-sovereign-projects.

The challenges in implementing the region's infrastructure projects suggests that further efforts could be made in improving co-ordination and institutional capacities. Key areas of concerns for Emerging Asian countries include strengthening co-ordination within government and across levels of government in the country, using project-appropriate arrangements with private sector partners, and regularising means of communication and co-ordination with international partners on regional and other cross-border initiatives.

Limitations in technical capacities and governance challenges more generally, which could be improved upon in the region, can inhibit the timely delivery of planned infrastructure projects. In 2016, 9 of the 12 Emerging Asian countries – all except Brunei Darussalam, Malaysia and Singapore – were ranked in the bottom half of the world in three or more of the Worldwide Governance Indicators categories (voice and accountability, political stability and absence of violence/terrorism, government effectiveness, regulatory quality, rule of law and control of corruption) (World Bank, 2018a). Good governance is needed at all stages of the life cycle of infrastructure assets: needs evaluation; decision and prioritisation of projects; project preparation; construction; and operation, delivery and maintenance. Governance preconditions, in turn, include a long-term national strategic vision for infrastructure use, appropriate regulatory frameworks, user-centric processes for managing projects, assessment mechanisms, transparency and anti-corruption mechanisms, and comprehensive consideration of appropriate delivery modalities (OECD, 2015).

Effective co-ordination is also needed across levels of government, which often have complementary responsibilities in planning and implementing infrastructure investments. Public investment is a major component of sub-national spending in many Emerging Asian countries, accounting for 39.6% of sub-national government expenditure in Thailand, 32.4% in China and 27.8% in Viet Nam (OECD/UCLG, 2016). Since investment needs differ among sub-national regions, local and regional governments should pursue differentiated investment strategies. Multi-level governance of public investment can be hindered by co-ordination challenges, capacity challenges and challenges in framework conditions (OECD, 2012a). Both vertical co-ordination across levels of government and horizontal co-ordination among sub-national governments are important in increasing efficiency through economies of scale and enhancing synergies. Capacity development and the implementation of good governance principles at all levels are also likely to be important actions. Private-sector partners help to finance and improve the implementation and operation of infrastructure projects; over 2010-14, private infrastructure investment accounted for 38.9% of investment in India, and 19.2% in Southeast Asia (ADB, 2017b). However, managing these projects can be challenging for governments. Consideration should be given to factors including project identification, risk management, government capacities in assessment and monitoring, and interaction between public–private partnerships and other policy tools (OECD, 2012b). If it is determined that private-sector participation can provide better value for money, the selection of appropriate PPP arrangements to match project characteristics is critical in managing risks. Over 2013-17, the most common form of arrangement was build-operate-transfer (BOT), in which governments bear equity risks, and private partners bear risks associated with construction; these accounted for 43.4% of infrastructure projects in Emerging Asia with private-sector participation (Figure 1.32). BOT projects have also become relatively more common over time; they accounted for only 30.5% of projects during 1993-97. Also common in the region in recent years are build-own-operate (23.1%) and build-rehabilitate-operate-transfer arrangements (10.3%).

Regional and cross-border infrastructure projects are progressing; the various initiatives need to be aligned with domestic infrastructure strategies and implementation capacities. ASEAN co-operation on infrastructure is directed by the *Master Plan on ASEAN Connectivity 2025*, which was adopted at the 28th ASEAN Summit in Vientiane, Lao PDR in September 2016. The master plan identifies five strategic areas in pursuing improved physical, institutional and people-to-people connectivity: sustainable infrastructure, digital innovation, seamless logistics, regulatory excellence and people mobility. Large projects being implemented and considered include the ASEAN Highway Network, the Singapore-Kunming Rail Link, the ASEAN Roll-on/Roll-off (RO-RO) Shipping Network and Short-Sea Shipping, the ASEAN Power Grid, the Trans-ASEAN Gas Pipeline and the ASEAN Broadband Corridor. The ASEAN Infrastructure Fund promotes the financing of regional infrastructure. In addition, infrastructure issues are addressed in larger regional frameworks, such as the East Asia Summit and ASEAN-Australia Infrastructure Co-operation Initiative, and sub-regional frameworks, such as the Greater Mekong Subregion. Countries in the region are also participating in the Belt and Road Initiative. Given the delays that have often faced international co-operation on infrastructure projects and strategies, such efforts can be made more effective through regularised means of communication such as ministry-level focal points or periodic consultation meetings on recent developments (OECD, 2016).

Figure 1.32. **Public-private partnership (PPP) projects in Emerging Asia by type, 2013-17**

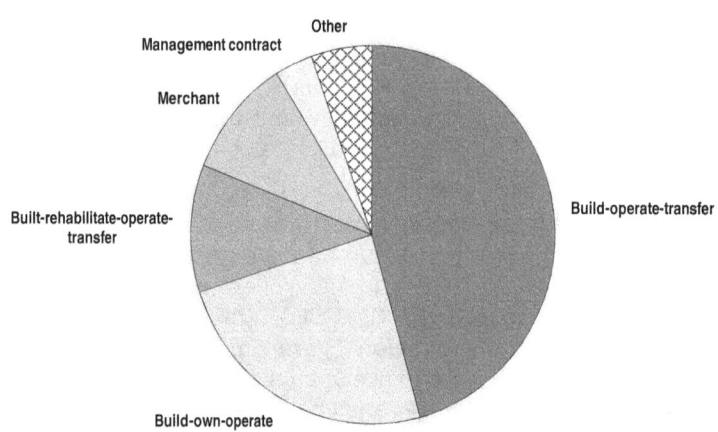

Note: These results were compiled from a non-exhaustive database of projects with private sector participation. No data are available for projects with private participation in Brunei Darussalam, Myanmar or Singapore.
Source: World Bank (2018b), *Private Participation in Infrastructure Database*, https://ppi.worldbank.org.
StatLink https://doi.org/10.1787/888933800233

Regional integration needs to be strengthened further amidst rising protectionism

Global trade growth will be decreasing in the near term

World trade has been growing since the end of 2016, and it expanded even further throughout 2017. This signalled the rebound of the global economy, which had been in a malaise in the previous years. On average, global trade grew by 4.7% in 2017, marking its highest level in six years, compared with a mere 1.5% in 2016 and a promising 2.1% in 2015, according to the World Trade Organization (WTO). Also in 2017, the growth of global trade overtook that of global gross domestic product (GDP) for the first time since 2011.

WTO projected that merchandise trade volume is poised to grow by 4.4% in 2018. Trade growth is expected to reach 4.0% in 2019, significantly lower than the mean of 4.8% observed since 1990, although still far above the post-crisis average of 3.0%. However, pronounced trade tensions and rising protectionism in terms of tariff hikes on some goods are affecting business confidence and investment decisions, and this would have an impact on global trade growth (WTO, 2018).

Tariffs have been cut on more than 90% of ASEAN products

All members of the Association of Southeast Asian Nations (Brunei Darussalam, Cambodia, Indonesia, Lao PDR, Malaysia, Myanmar, the Philippines, Singapore, Thailand and Viet Nam) have progressed significantly in reducing tariffs. Eliminating non-tariff barriers can increase intra-regional trade among ASEAN members; strengthening trade-facilitation efforts, which have been going on for the past few years, can help reduce or eliminate these barriers.

ASEAN trade is very much liberalised, with significant and drastic tariff reductions on many products for both ASEAN members and non-members. ASEAN members offer preferential tariffs to non-members on a most-favoured-nation (MFN) basis. The message is clear: to be part of ASEAN means to be open to trade, not just with other members, but also with all countries. More than 90.0% of ASEAN members' tariff lines have a preference margin of zero, where preferential tariffs are no lower than the MFN rate. More than 70.0% of intra-regional trade is conducted at zero-rated MFN rates. ASEAN rarely uses preferences (Menon, 2018). ASEAN multilateralisation has resulted in a lower share of intra-regional trade, never surpassing 25.0% of the region's total trade. However, ASEAN has successfully promoted rapid growth for its members since the start of the ASEAN Free Trade Agreement.

ASEAN is the fourth-largest exporting region in the world, behind only the European Union (EU), North America and China. ASEAN accounts for just 3.3% of global GDP, but it produces more than 7.0% of global exports due to its involvement in global value chains. If intra-regional trade is to increase, it should be fuelled by factors other than preferential tariffs, such as the elimination of non-tariff barriers. Presently, the use of non-tariff measures (NTMs) is prevalent among ASEAN member countries. In 2015, it was recorded that all ASEAN countries implemented all types of technical measures, which include sanitary and phytosanitary measures (SPS), technical barriers to trade (TBT), and pre-shipment inspection and other formalities. All countries have also used non-technical measures, which cover non-automatic licensing; quotas; prohibitions and quantity control measures other than for SPS or TBT; and price-control measures, including additional taxes and charges (Table 1.8).

Table 1.8. **Non-tariff measures recorded in 2015 for ASEAN members**

Non-Tariff measures	BND	IDN	THA	SGP	MYS	PHL	VNM	KHM	LAO	MYA
Technical measures										
A. Sanitary and phytosanitary measures and B. Technical barriers to trade and C. Pre-shipment inspection and other formalities	X	X	X	X	X	X	X	X	X	X
Non-technical measures										
E. Non-automatic licensing, quotas, prohibitions and quantity control measures other than for SPS or TBT	X	X	X	X	X	X	X	X	X	X
F. Price-control measures, including additional taxes and charges	X	X	X	X	X	X	X	X	X	X
G. Finance measures						X	X		X	
H. Measures affecting competition		X	X			X	X			X
Exports										
P Export-related measures	X	X	X	X	X	X	X	X	X	X

Note: WITS database notes that information on NTMs can be outdated and only partially reported.
Source: OECD Development Centre based on World Bank (2018c), WITS database, http://wits.worldbank.org/witsavailabletarifftypes.

The CLMV countries (Cambodia, Lao PDR, Myanmar and Viet Nam), are required to further reduce tariffs on additional products by 2018. As a result, thousands of goods will enjoy a 0% import tariff by the end of 2018. This is very much in line with Viet Nam's commitments on special preferential import duty rates, within the framework of its ten existing free-trade agreements (FTAs). Lao PDR, Myanmar and Cambodia are due to further reduce tariffs on remaining products by the end of 2018; this would mark the achievement of a level playing field for all ASEAN members. On 5 January 2018, Viet Nam introduced ten decrees concerning preferential import tariffs for 2018-23. This tariff reduction affects free-trade deals such as ASEAN, ASEAN-China, ASEAN-Korea, ASEAN-Japan, ASEAN-India, ASEAN-Australia-New Zealand, Viet Nam-Japan, Viet Nam-Korea, Viet Nam-Chile and Viet Nam-Eurasian Economic Union (EAEU).

Notes

1. Growth rates are computed based on series in real prices and on a year-on-year annual basis unless specified otherwise.
2. Core inflation in defined differently across Emerging Asian economies. Generally, it excludes fresh food and/or other volatile food prices, as well as goods and services whose prices are administered (e.g. electricity, fuel and light petroleum gas), although the specific subcomponents excluded in the measure are different in each country. One exception to the generally accepted rule is Singapore, where the measure of core inflation excludes private road transport and accommodation.
3. *Shari'a* commercial banks and business units are banks following the principles of Islamic finance.
4. Infrastructure quality rankings are not available for Myanmar in the most recent edition of The Global Competitiveness Report. Rankings are available for 137 economies.

References

ADB (2018a), *Asian Development Outlook 2018: How Technology Affects Jobs*, Asian Development Bank, Manila, www.adb.org/sites/default/files/publication/411666/ado2018.pdf

ADB (2108b), *ADB Sovereign Projects* (database), Asian Development Bank, Manila, https://data.adb.org/dataset/adb-sovereign-projects

ADB (2017a), *2017 Development Effectiveness Review*, Asian Development Bank, Manila, www.adb.org/sites/default/files/institutional-document/418291/defr-2017-main-report.pdf

ADB (2017b), *Meeting Asia's Infrastructure Needs*, Asian Development Bank, Manila, www.adb.org/sites/default/files/publication/227496/special-report-infrastructure.pdf

ADB (2015), *Cambodia's Special Economic Zones*, Asian Development Bank, Manila, https://www.adb.org/sites/default/files/publication/175236/ewp-459.pdf

Aizenman, J., Y.W. Cheung and H. Ito (2017), "The Interest Rate Effect on Private Saving: Alternative Perspectives", *ADBI Working Papers*, No. 715, Asian Development Bank Institute, Tokyo, www.adb.org/sites/default/files/publication/239546/adbi-wp715.pdf.

Anaya, P., M. Hachula and C.J. Offermanns (2017), "Spillovers of U.S. Unconventional Monetary Policy to Emerging Markets: The Role of Capital Flows", *Journal of International Money and Finance*, Vol 73, Part B, Elsevier, Amsterdam, pp. 275-295.

ASEAN (2017), *ASEAN Investment Report 2017*, ASEAN Secretariat, Jakarta, http://asean.org/storage/2017/11/ASEAN-Investment-Report-2017.pdf.

BIS (2018a), "Total credit to non-financial corporations", *BIS Statistics* (database), Bank for International Settlements, Basel, https://stats.bis.org/.

BIS (2018b), "Total credit to households & NPISHs", *BIS Statistics* (database), Bank for International Settlements, Basel, https://stats.bis.org/.

BIS (2018c), "Nominal EER indices", *BIS Statistics* (database), Bank for International Settlements, Basel, https://stats.bis.org/.

Borodin, K. and A. Strokov (2011), "Central Banks' Interest Rate and International Trade in BRIC countries: Agriculture vs Machinery Industry?", Conference Paper, Leibniz-Institut für Agrarentwicklung in Mittel- und Osteuropa (IAMO) Forum 2011, No. 18, Halle, www.econstor.eu/bitstream/10419/50792/1/670800821.pdf

Chen, Q., A. Filardo, D. He and F. Zhu (2015), "Financial crisis, US Unconventional Monetary Policy and International Spillovers", *BIS Working Papers*, No. 494, Bank for International Settlements, Basel, www.bis.org/publ/work494.pdf.

DOF (2018a), "Tax Reform for Acceleration and Inclusion (TRAIN), Package 1A (RA 10963)", Philippines Department of Finance, Manila, https://manila2018.dof.gov.ph/wp-content/uploads/2018/02/TRAIN-Package-1-Grand-Presentation.pdf (accessed on 1 July 2018).

DOF (2018b), "What is TRAIN? Tax Reform for Acceleration and Inclusion", Philippines Department of Finance, Manila, www.dof.gov.ph/taxreform/index.php/pit/ (accessed on 1 July 2018).

Fusion Media Ltd (2018), *Government Bond Yields, Nominal Exchange Rate and Stock Market Indices* (database), www.investing.com.

Global Infrastructure Hub (2018), *Infrastructure Outlook* (database), Global Infrastructure Hub, Sydney, https://outlook.gihub.org.

Gupta, S., E. Liu and C. Mulas-Garanados (2015), "Now or later? The political economy of public investment in democracies", *IMF Working Paper*, No. 175, International Monetary Fund, Washington, D.C., www.imf.org/external/pubs/ft/wp/2015/wp15175.pdf

IMF (2018a), "Lao People's Democratic Republic : 2017 Article IV Consultation-Press Release; Staff Report; and Statement by the Executive Director for Lao People's Democratic Republic", International Monetary Fund, Washington, DC, www.imf.org/en/Publications/CR/Issues/2018/03/23/Lao-Peoples-Democratic-Republic-2017-Article-IV-Consultation-Press-Release-Staff-Report-and-45750.

IMF (2018b), *International Financial Statistics* (database), International Monetary Fund, Washington, D.C., http://data.imf.org/?sk=4C514D48-B6BA-49ED-8AB9-52B0C1A0179B.

Kapoor, M. and S. Ravi (2009), *The Effect of Interest Rate on Household Consumption: Evidence from a Natural Experiment in India*, American Economic Association 2010 Annual Meeting Papers, www.aeaweb.org/conference/2010/2010_AEA_meeting_papers.php.

Keimling, N. (2018), "Stock Market Valuation: Fundamental Valuation Ratios in International Equity Markets", www.starcapital.de/en/research/stock-market-valuation/ (accessed 20 June 2018).

Menon, J. (2018), "ASEAN's new challenge: lower non-tariff barriers to trade", *The Myanmar Times*, Yangon, www.mmtimes.com/news/aseans-new-challenge-lower-non-tariff-barriers-trade.html.

Miyajima, K., M.S. Mohanty and J. Yetman (2014), "Spillovers of US Unconventional Monetary Policy to Asia: The Role of Long-term Interest Rates", *BIS Working Papers, No. 478*, Bank for International Settlements, Basel, www.bis.org/publ/work478.pdf.

Mourougane, A., B. Jarmila, J. Fournier, N. Pain and E. Rusticelli (2016), "Can an increase in public investment sustainable lift economic growth?", *OECD Economics Department Working Papers*, No. 1351, OECD Publishing, Paris, www.oecd.org/eco/Can-an-increase-in-public-investment-sustainably-lift-economic-growth.pdf

OECD (2018), *OECD FDI Regulatory Restrictiveness Index*, OECD Publishing, Paris, http://www.oecd.org/investment/fdiindex.htm.

OECD (2017a), *Economic Outlook for Southeast Asia, China and India 2017: Addressing Energy Challenges*, OECD Publishing, Paris, http://dx.doi.org/10.1787/saeo-2017-en.

OECD (2017b), *Revenue Statistics in Asian Countries 2017: Trends in Indonesia, Japan, Kazakhstan, Korea, Malaysia, the Philippines and Singapore*, OECD Publishing, Paris, www.oecd.org/ctp/revenue-statistics-in-asian-countries-2017-9789264278943-en.htm.

OECD (2016), *Economic Outlook for Southeast Asia, China and India 2016: Enhancing Regional Ties*, OECD Publishing, Paris, http://dx.doi.org/10.1787/saeo-2016-en.

OECD (2015), *Towards a Framework for the Governance of Infrastructure*, OECD Publishing, Paris, www.oecd.org/gov/budgeting/Towards-a-Framework-for-the-Governance-of-Infrastructure.pdf

OECD (2012a), *Recommendation of the Council on Effective Public Investment across Levels of Government*, OECD Publishing, Paris, www.oecd.org/regional/regional-policy/Principles-Public-Investment.pdf

OECD (2012b), *Recommendations of the Council on Principles for Public Governance of Public-Private Partnerships*, OECD Publishing, Paris, www.oecd.org/governance/budgeting/PPP-Recommendation.pdf

OECD/UCLG (2016), *Subnational Governments around the world: Structure and finance*, OECD Publishing, Paris, www.oecd.org/gov/budgeting/Towards-a-Framework-for-the-Governance-of-Infrastructure.pdf

Okeyo, M. P., C. M. Rambo, P. A. Odundo (2015), "Effects of delayed payment of contractors on the completion of infrastructural projects: A case of Sondu-Miriu Hydropower Project, Kisumu County, Kenya", *Chinese Business Review*, Vol. 14/7, pp. 325-336.

Oosterhaven, J. and T. Knaap (2003), "Spatial economic impacts of transport infrastructure investments" in *Transport Projects, Programmes, and Policies*, Interdisciplinary Centre for Comparative Research in the Social Sciences, Farnham, www.rug.nl/staff/j.oosterhaven/transtalk03%20raem%20zzl.pdf

Punzi, M.T. (2018), "Integrative Report: Household Debt in SEACEN Economies", in *Household Debt in SEACEN Economies*, The South East Asian Central Banks (SEACEN) Research and Training Centre, Kuala Lumpur, www.seacen.org/publications/RePEc/702001-100437-PDF.pdf.

Punzi, M.T. and P. Chantapacdepong (2017), "Spillover Effects of Unconventional Monetary Policy in Asia and the Pacific Region", *ADBI Working Papers, No. 630*, Asian Development Bank Institute, Tokyo, www.adb.org/sites/default/files/publication/220146/adbi-wp630.pdf.

RBI (2017), "Financial Stability Report December 2017, Issue No. 16", Reserve Bank of India, Mumbai, https://rbidocs.rbi.org.in/rdocs/PublicationReport/Pdfs/0FSR201730210986ADDA44E2A946A3F6C4408581.PDF.

Sambasivan, M. and Y. W. Soon (2007), "Causes and effects of delays in Malaysian construction industry", *International Journal of Project Management*, Vol. 25, pp. 517-526.

WEF (2017), *The Global Competitiveness Report 2017-2018*, World Economic Forum, Geneva, https://www.weforum.org/reports/the-global-competitiveness-report-2017-2018.

Weisblatt, B. et. al. (2018), "Vietnam Strategy 2018: Well positioned to thrive on global appetites", *Viet Capital Securities*, www.vcsc.com.vn/userfiles/others/VietnamStrategy2018-20180105.pdf.

World Bank (2018a), *Worldwide Governance Indicators* (database), World Bank, Washington, DC, http://info.worldbank.org/governance/wgi.

World Bank (2018b), *Private Participation in Infrastructure Database*, World Bank, Washington, DC, https://ppi.worldbank.org.

World Bank (2018c), *World Integrated Trade Solution* (database), World Bank, Washington DC, https://wits.worldbank.org.

WTO (2018), "Trade statistics and outlook: Strong trade growth in 2018 rests on policy choices", World Trade Organization, Geneva, www.wto.org/english/news_e/pres18_e/pr820_e.pdf (accessed on 1 July 2018).

Chapter 2

Emerging Asia in the era of cross-border e-commerce

> E-commerce is becoming increasingly important around the world and Emerging Asia, and China in particular, is already playing a major role in this form of economic activity. While the e-commerce market remains smaller than traditional markets, further growth in e-commerce is expected in the future in the region and globally. The scale of e-commerce in the region and the potential for its further development are the result of multiple factors, including levels of ICT use, the development of ICT infrastructure, transportation infrastructure and logistics capabilities, the use of e-commerce payment systems, and the legal and regulatory environment. Among the most important policy areas to be addressed in fostering its continued development are improvements in connectivity, the development of digital skills and the provision of digital security.

Introduction

The rapid expansion of electronic commerce (e-commerce) is radically altering our society. More and more economic activities use the Internet and new information and communication technology (ICT) tools to do business or to purchase goods and services on line. These interactions and transactions can take place between governments, businesses and consumers (Table 2.1). Of particular interest are the cross-border business-to-business (B2B) and business-to-consumer (B2C) transactions that look set to drastically reshape trade and business in Emerging Asia (Emerging Asia is comprised of the ten members of the Association of Southeast Asian Nations – Brunei Darussalam, Cambodia, Indonesia, Lao PDR, Malaysia, Myanmar, the Philippines, Singapore, Thailand and Viet Nam – plus China and India).

Table 2.1. **Forms of e-commerce and other Internet applications**

	Government	Business	Consumer
Government	G2G (e.g. co-ordination)	G2B (e.g. information)	G2C (e.g. information)
Business	B2G (e.g. procurement)	B2B (e.g. e-commerce)	B2C (e.g. e-commerce)
Consumer	C2G (e.g. tax compliance)	C2B (e.g. price comparison)	C2C (e.g. auction markets)

Source: OECD (2000), *OECD Economic Outlook* No. 67.

Global cross-border e-commerce is increasingly important in the international economy. It has introduced new dynamics to international trade. Cross-border business-to-business (B2B) e-commerce, for example, typically involves fewer intermediate links between sellers and buyers, but it places higher demands on services, especially information, payment and logistics.

E-commerce growth in Emerging Asia has been rapid, particularly in China. China is the world's largest B2C e-commerce market and among the frontrunners of cross-border e-commerce. Furthermore, relatively new business models – such as an online market combined with a brick-and-mortar store – are emerging, and sellers and buyers are increasingly adopting them. As a result, e-commerce continues to evolve and open up more opportunities. The following sections explore the e-commerce trends and market outlook for Emerging Asia, the factors that are affecting its growth – including the use of ICT, the level of development of ICT infrastructure, the quality of transportation infrastructure and logistics services, the availability of e-payment systems, and legal and regulatory environments, and followed by policy options for supporting the development of e-commerce in the region. Governments in the region have important roles to play in facilitating the growth of e-commerce through addressing some important policy areas including improvements in connectivity, development of digital skills and provision of digital security.

Cross-border e-commerce trends and outlook

Cross-border B2B e-commerce has been growing steadily since the 1990s. Growth accelerated in the 21st century with the expansion and deepening of global value chains (GVCs). While B2B still dominates cross-border e-commerce, international B2C e-commerce has been growing quickly. The business sector in Emerging Asia has been adapting quickly to this new environment. In most countries in the region, ICT use in business transactions was above the world average in 2014-16 (Figure 2.1). Only Cambodia, Lao PDR and Myanmar lag behind. India's score is also below the world average.

Figure 2.1. **ICT use in B2B and B2C transactions, 2014-16**
Index, scale 1-7 from lowest to highest level of ICT use

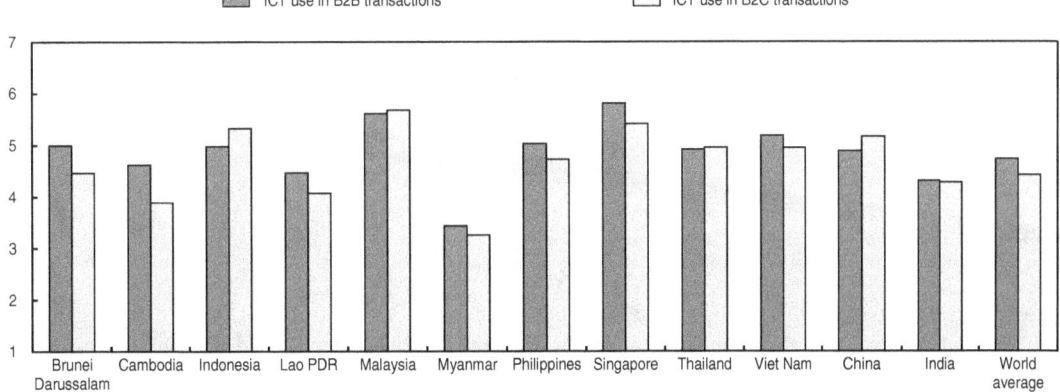

Note: The score is based on the view of firm executives interviewed in the WEF (2017) Executive Opinion Survey.
Source: WEF (2017), Executive Opinion Survey.
StatLink https://doi.org/10.1787/888933800252

Further growth is expected in the future. From 2015 to 2021, the region's total B2C e-commerce market revenue is expected to increase from about USD 320 billion (US dollars) to more than USD 900 billion. China's market will contribute more than 90% of the growth; the country's share in the global e-commerce market will increase from about 30% in 2015 to nearly 40% in 2021. India and ASEAN will increase their combined weight in the global market from 2.5% to 4% (Figure 2.2).

Figure 2.2. **E-commerce market revenue, 2015-21**

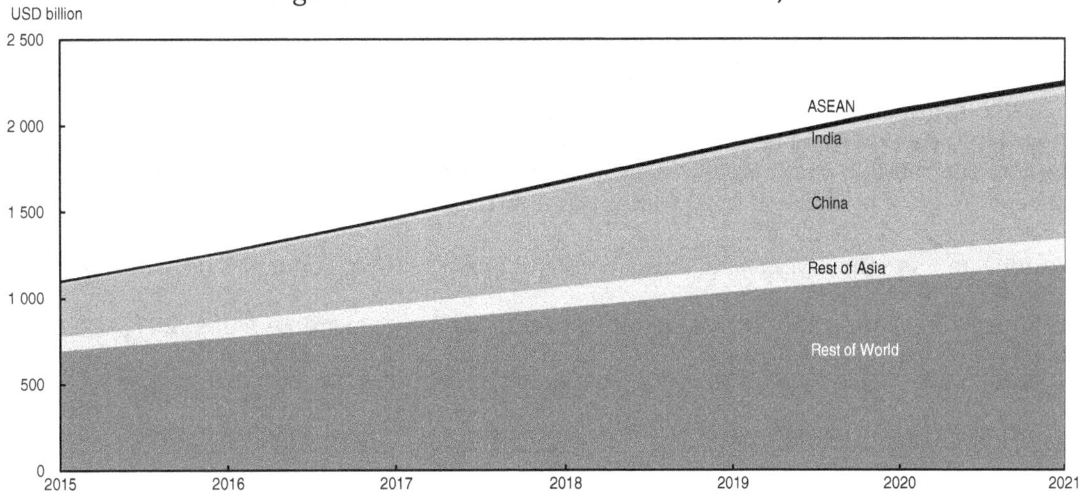

Source: Statista.
StatLink https://doi.org/10.1787/888933799587

Emerging Asia also accounts for a disproportionate share of Internet and e-commerce users. The region accounted for 50% of the world's Internet population in 2015, which was greater than its share of the world's total population. In 2015, ASEAN, China and India had 681.2 million e-commerce users; the number is projected to nearly double by 2021 (Figure 2.3). Emerging Asia will host about 60% of global Internet users by the end of 2021; a large population with Internet access allows Asian markets to play a significant role in global e-commerce activities. The number of Internet users in India is expected to increase from nearly 400 million in 2015 to more than 600 million in 2021, accounting for almost one-quarter of the region's total Internet population. ASEAN's average Internet penetration rate will surpass 60%, spurred by the boom of Internet users in Indonesia and the Philippines. During this period, China's Internet users will grow by about 6% per year, although its average annual population growth rate is less than 0.4%.

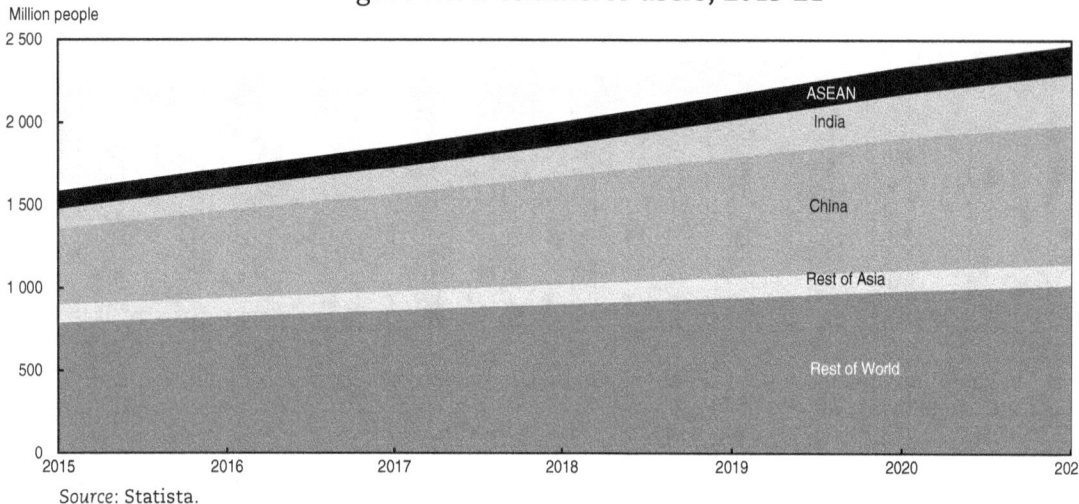

Figure 2.3. **E-commerce users, 2015-21**

Source: Statista.
StatLink https://doi.org/10.1787/888933799606

The global e-commerce market remains smaller than traditional markets, but is growing quickly. In the next five years, global e-commerce is projected to account for about two-fifths of the increase in private consumption (BCG, 2014). B2C e-commerce sales are expected to grow by 20% or more on average every year, much higher than the 4% annual growth rate for traditional retail sales, though traditional transactions will still make up a much larger share of the total retail market. The share of online sales in total revenue has continued to increase in recent years.

B2C e-commerce in most Emerging Asian markets is expected to record double-digit growth in the next five to ten years. From 2016 to 2021, the world's three fastest-growing markets for retail e-commerce will be Malaysia, India and Indonesia; all three are expected to grow by more than 20% annually (Statista, 2016). By 2021, the size of India's e-commerce market will be larger than that of ASEAN. Retail e-commerce in China will continue growing rapidly, as well, with an annual growth rate of about 17% (Figure 2.4).

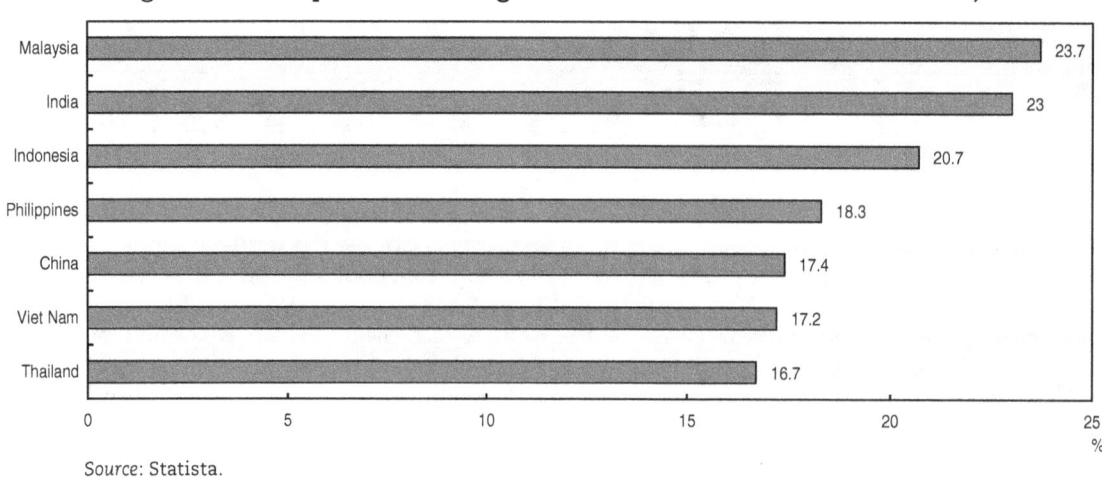

Figure 2.4. **Compound annual growth rate of B2C e-commerce sales, 2016-21**

Source: Statista.
StatLink https://doi.org/10.1787/888933800271

Factors affecting the growth of cross-border e-commerce

These trends are the result of multiple factors. Improvements to ICT technologies that increase their usefulness and lower costs have been a major driver of global e-commerce growth. Economies of scale and positive externalities from network effects are also lowering the costs of e-commerce and making its platforms more attractive as they grow. At the same time, the strength of B2C e-commerce in Emerging Asia is connected to a general increase in consumption in much of the region as a result of longer-term structural factors such as rising incomes and expanding middle classes.

Of greater interest to policy makers in the region are the more proximate and malleable factors that have been and will continue to drive e-commerce in Emerging Asia. These factors include the use of new technologies, the level of development of ICT infrastructure, the quality of transportation infrastructure and logistics services, the availability and reliability of e-payment systems, and legal and regulatory environments. These drivers have gone through rapid change in recent years and are significantly different across the region.

ICT use

In the long run, economic digitalisation tends to improve Asian countries' adaptability to the world economy and facilitates their integration into GVCs. The use of digital technologies increases efficiency. For instance, it helps producers and service providers create and enlarge markets, lower operating costs, facilitate transactions and improve competitiveness. Digital technologies offer consumers more information and choice, easier ways to purchase and a higher quality of services. Alongside the development of e-commerce systems, ICT is also being used in the region in providing e-government tools to improve governance generally (Box 2.1).

Box 2.1. E-government in Emerging Asia

To assess the quality and usefulness of information and services that a country provides to society using ICT tools, the United Nations developed the E-Participation Index (Figure 2.5). This measures the quality, relevance and usefulness of governmental efforts (including websites and online databases) to provide online information and participatory tools and services. The value of the index ranges from zero to one. A higher score means a higher quality of e-government services.

Figure 2.5. E-Participation Index, 2012 and 2016
Index, scale 0-1 from lowest to highest level of participation

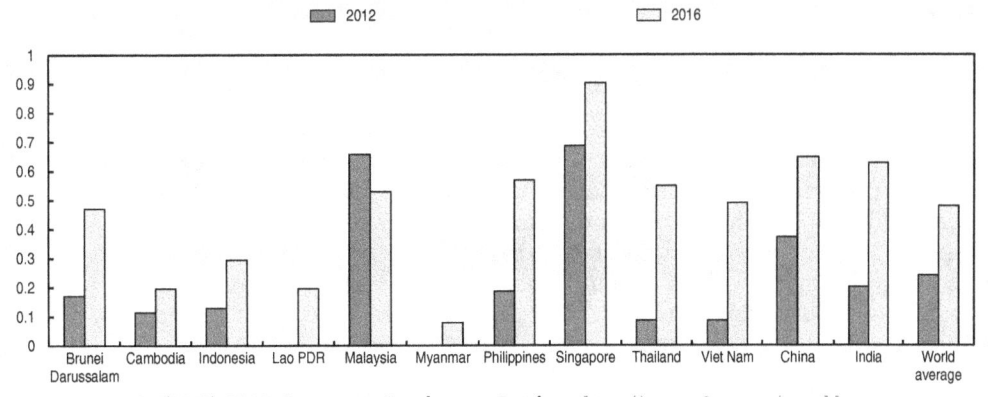

Source: UNDESA (2018), UN E-Government Development Database, http://unpan3.un.org/egovkb.
StatLink https://doi.org/10.1787/888933800290

> **Box 2.1. E-government in Emerging Asia** *(cont.)*
>
> The world's average level of e-participation increased from 0.24 in 2012 to 0.48 in 2016. The evolution of Emerging Asian countries' scores from 2012 to 2016 shows the region's efforts to improve public services using digital technologies. In 2012, only China, Malaysia and Singapore had scores higher than the world average; in 2016, most countries' scores surpassed the world average. Cambodia, Lao PDR and Myanmar's scores were still relatively low, though they have progressed significantly. This is due mainly to capacity rather than willingness. The 2000 e-ASEAN Framework Agreement recommends enabling "Member States who are ready to accelerate the implementation of this Agreement to assist other Member States to undertake capacity building" (ASEAN, 2000).

The percentage of the population using the Internet has risen steadily across the region in recent years, although there are still significant differences between countries. In high-income countries like Singapore and Brunei Darussalam, as well as middle-income Malaysia the figure is higher than in other countries in the region (Figure 2.6). Despite its vibrant services sector in IT, India has a low rate of Internet use, with little more than a quarter of the population going on line. This reflects difficulties in bringing infrastructure and services to populations outside the main centres, and in doing so at a cost that poor consumers find reasonable (OECD, 2018).

Figure 2.6. **Internet users as a percentage of population, 2000-16**

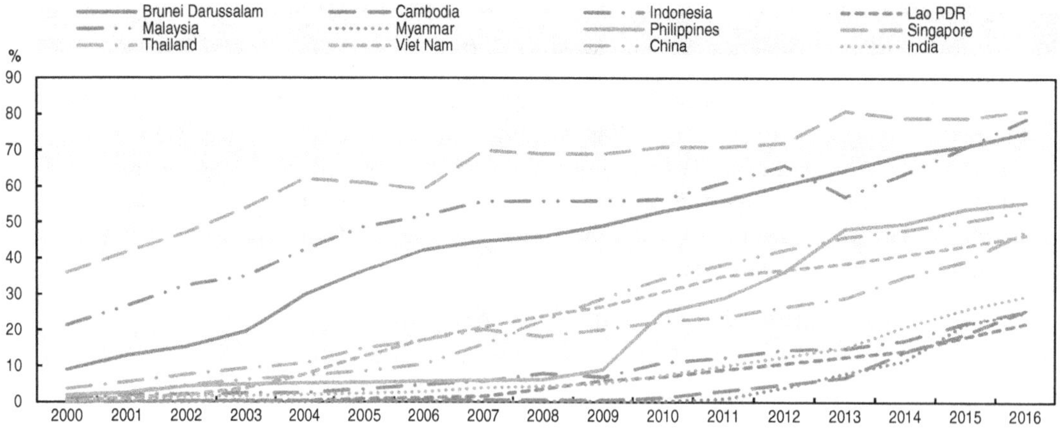

Source: World Bank (2017), *World Development Indicators*.
StatLink https://doi.org/10.1787/888933799625

Firms in Emerging Asia have been relatively quick adopters of the new technologies needed to participate in cross-border e-commerce. To some extent, the region's adaptability to global economic digitalisation comes from its capacity in technology adoption and incremental innovation. First, deep involvement in GVCs allows Emerging Asia to access the latest technologies and facilitates its learning. Second, countries' capacity in incremental innovation allows them to benefit from second-mover advantages to grow faster and even jump the market frontier; examples are e-payment's popularity in China and the Alibaba Group's success.

New technologies have been adopted by and incorporated into the operations of many Emerging Asian firms, and have already had significant consequences on business activity, trade and productivity in the region (OECD, 2018). According to the Executive

Opinion Survey conducted by the World Economic Forum (WEF), businesses in Emerging Asia – particularly those in China, Indonesia, Malaysia and Thailand – have managed to adopt the latest ICTs to link with the global market (Table 2.2). Many business leaders believe that digitalisation will introduce new business and organisational models to the region (WEF, 2017). It allows, for instance, more integrated and interactively-connected production and distribution processes through digital networks (OECD, 2018).

Table 2.2. **Firm-level technology adoption in ASEAN, China and India, 2007-17**
Index, scale 1-7 from lowest to highest level of technology use

Country	2007-08	2008-09	2009-10	2010-11	2011-12	2012-13	2013-14	2014-15	2015-16	2016-17
Brunei Darussalam	n.a.	5.07	4.96	4.82	4.86	4.85	4.78	n.a.	n.a.	4.37
Cambodia	4.15	4.13	4.42	4.43	4.70	4.86	4.59	4.27	4.27	4.20
Indonesia	4.70	4.79	4.81	4.88	4.98	4.95	5.08	5.06	5.06	5.00
Lao PDR	n.a.	n.a.	n.a.	n.a.	n.a.	n.a.	4.47	4.30	4.30	4.11
Malaysia	5.78	5.61	5.39	5.49	5.59	5.56	5.46	5.58	5.58	5.46
Myanmar	n.a.	n.a.	n.a.	n.a.	n.a.	n.a.	2.73	2.94	2.94	n.a.
Philippines	4.94	5.11	5.06	4.98	5.06	5.17	5.22	5.07	5.07	4.70
Singapore	6.05	5.99	6.03	5.96	5.97	6.02	5.83	5.71	5.71	5.67
Thailand	5.16	4.88	4.91	4.88	4.73	4.98	5.02	4.86	4.86	4.92
Viet Nam	5.08	5.07	5.08	4.96	4.56	3.98	3.76	3.89	3.89	4.38
ASEAN average	5.12	5.08	5.08	5.05	5.06	5.05	4.69	4.63	4.63	4.76
China	5.00	5.15	5.14	4.95	4.91	4.75	4.69	4.66	4.66	4.60
India	5.58	5.52	5.47	5.32	5.28	5.24	5.05	4.19	4.19	4.36
Emerging Asia average	5.16	5.13	5.13	5.07	5.06	5.04	4.72	4.59	4.59	4.71

Notes: n.a. = not available.
Source: WEF (2017), *Executive Opinion Survey*.

Engagement in e-commerce varies both within and across countries in the region, with smaller firms less likely to take part in e-commerce, for example. In Singapore, 47.6% of firms reported receiving orders over the Internet in 2014, with 42.9% of micro enterprises (zero to nine employees) and 54.6% of large enterprises (250 or more employees) using the Internet in this way (Figure 2.7). In Indonesia, where 24.6% of firms received orders over the Internet, differences by firm size were even greater, with 3.7% of micro enterprises reporting Internet orders, compared with 54.6% of large enterprises. In Thailand in 2013, 1.7% of businesses received Internet orders, ranging from 1.4% among micro enterprises to 14.7% among large enterprises.

Figure 2.7. **Proportion of businesses receiving orders over the Internet by size, 2014**

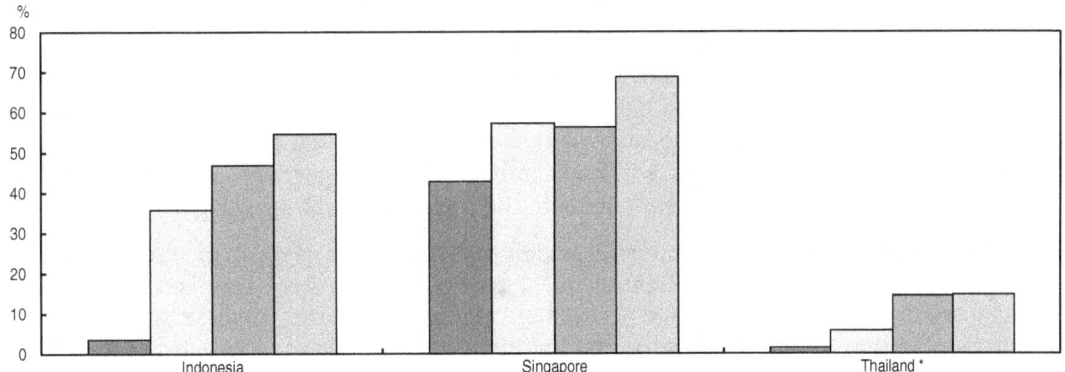

Note: (*) Thailand data is from 2013, the most recent year available.
Source: UNCTAD (2017), UNCTADSTAT (database), http://unctadstat.unctad.org.
StatLink https://doi.org/10.1787/888933800309

ICT infrastructure

E-commerce growth demands more stable, fast and affordable Internet connections. Increased Internet penetration and ICT improvements in the speed and capacity of online communications have spurred e-commerce growth. In general, Emerging Asian countries face challenges from development gaps across the region, especially between urban and rural areas. Wide development gaps persist despite Emerging Asian countries' efforts to expand ICT infrastructure. Poor broadband Internet connectivity in many Emerging Asian countries is due mainly to limited network coverage, slow Internet speeds, the high cost of connection and limited awareness (A.T. Kearney, 2015).

High-speed broadband Internet connections are critical in facilitating e-commerce. Factors like the use of broadband infrastructure and Internet technologies are also likely to enhance national aggregate outputs (Ng, Lye and Lim, 2013). However, Internet speeds are below the world average in many Emerging Asian countries (Table 2.3). Only Singapore and Thailand have higher shares of unique Internet Protocol version 4 (IPv4) addresses connecting at above 15 Mbps, while the rest of the region performs below the world average in all three speed categories, except for Viet Nam's connections that are above 4 Mbps. The gaps between the region and the world average seemed to widen at higher broadband speeds; this shows that Emerging Asia is still catching up in terms of ICT infrastructure.

Table 2.3. **IPv4 addresses by broadband connection speed in Emerging Asia, Q1 2017**

Country	% Above 4 Mbps	% Above 10 Mbps	% Above 15 Mbps
Indonesia	76 (71)	18 (68)	5 (69)
Malaysia	72 (80)	32 (52)	14 (52)
Philippines	39 (107)	11 (78)	6.2 (63)
Singapore	94 (17)	72 (4)	51 (6)
Thailand	97 (4)	72 (5)	43 (13)
Viet Nam	86 (49)	37 (48)	11 (57)
China	81 (59)	20 (62)	5 (70)
India	42 (104)	19 (64)	10 (58)
World average	82	45	28

Note: The number in the bracket indicates the country's global ranking.
Source: Akamai (2017), *State of the Internet Connectivity Report*.

In terms of technology, currently fibre-optic cables are the most efficient means to transmit data, despite the increased use of satellites. Even for mobile phones, the connection is wireless only between the device and the nearest mobile phone towers. Data is carried over terrestrial and subsea fibre-optic cables. Fibre networks are a crucial infrastructure for the digital economy. Building, maintaining and upgrading fibre networks require sustained inputs of capital, technology and managerial efforts. While these requirements pose common challenges to all countries worldwide, Emerging Asian countries face extra difficulties because of their highly dispersed geography and large populations. Financing challenges will need to be resolved, especially in capital-scarce countries. The lack of funding can contribute to the problem of urban-rural gaps in access.

Residents of Emerging Asian countries widely use mobile phones, and mobile network development has progressed significantly in the past decade. This enhances connectivity because more people are now able to access the Internet using smartphones. ASEAN has hundreds of millions of Internet users, and the majority of them are mobile-first Internet users, or people who access the web primarily through their mobile phones (eMarketer, 2016). Mobile technologies are becoming important components of global e-commerce (Box 2.2).

Box 2.2. Mobile Internet and e-commerce

E-commerce's new wave of growth is linked to the expansion of mobile broadband, the popularisation of smartphones, reduced costs for data usage, and rich online shopping and payment tools on portable devices and platforms. Almost 80% of Internet users in China and two-thirds of those in ASEAN use smartphones to access the Internet. The use of mobile phones is very widespread in Emerging Asia (Figure 2.8), with Thailand, Malaysia, Indonesia and Cambodia all enjoying similar levels of mobile phone usage as in high-income Singapore. Only Lao PDR stands out as having a much lower rate, at just over 50 subscriptions per 100 people. There is considerable evidence of catch-up growth within the region in the use of mobile phones. Singapore has been experiencing the slowest rate of growth while at the other end of the scale, some lower-income countries have seen explosive growth in the uptake of mobile phones since 2000, albeit from a relatively low base.

Figure 2.8. **Number and growth of mobile telephone subscriptions, 2000-15**

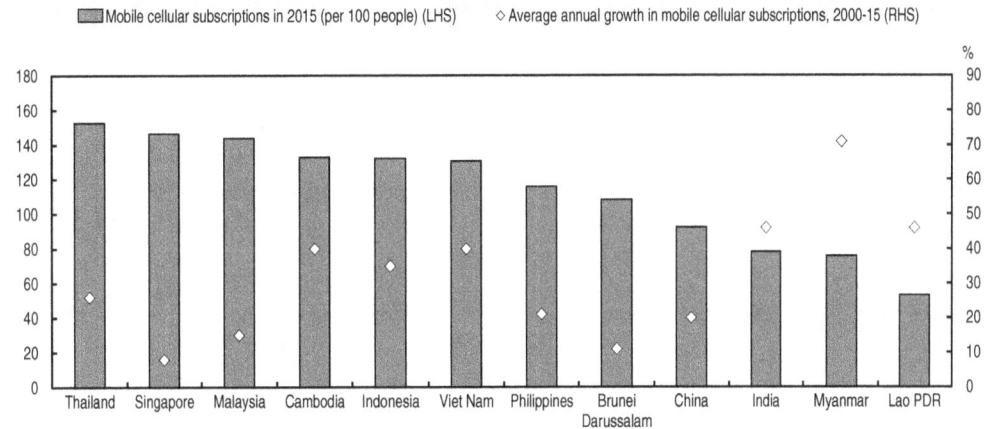

Source: World Bank (2017), *World Development Indicators*.
StatLink https://doi.org/10.1787/888933800328

This widespread use of smartphones can be one of the driving forces for e-commerce growth in Asia. A survey (Statista, 2016) of 30 000 owners of mobile connected devices across the world shows that 46% of respondents in Asia-Pacific use their mobile devices, mainly with mobile apps, to purchase products and services on line. This share is higher than that of Europe (32%) and North America (28%). The total revenue of the global mobile payment market in 2015 was estimated at USD 450 billion. The market is projected to expand by USD 150-170 billion per year, and to exceed USD 1 trillion by 2019. Smartphone access has accounted for more than half of visits to retail websites worldwide and about one-third of B2C revenues.

Accessible Internet means having both the physical infrastructure and an affordable price. The cost of broadband Internet remains relatively high across Emerging Asia, despite recent increases in Internet penetration (Figure 2.9). Fixed broadband prices exceed the affordability threshold of 5% of GNI in India, the Philippines, Indonesia, Lao PDR, Cambodia and Myanmar. In comparison, mobile broadband prices are below the affordability threshold in all countries in the region.

Figure 2.9. **Internet prices in Emerging Asia, 2015**
Percentage of gross national income per capita

Panel A. Fixed broadband

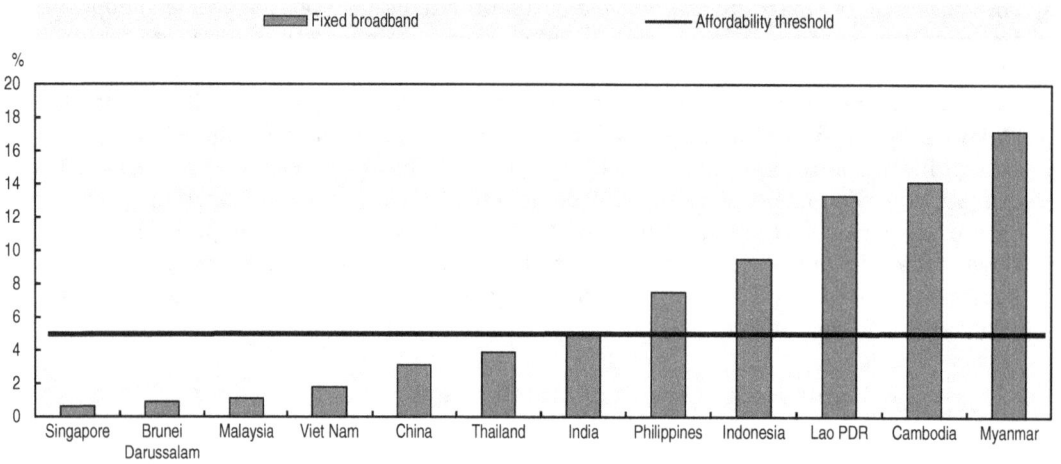

Panel B. Mobile broadband

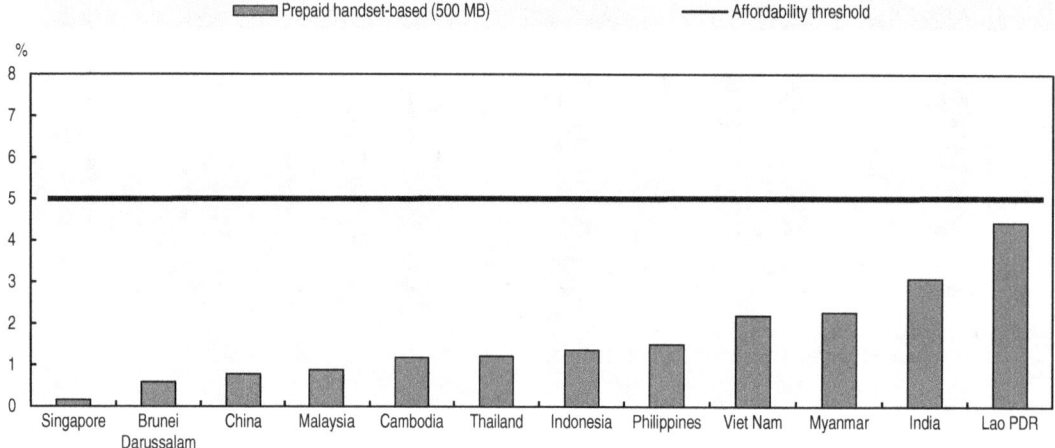

Note: The affordability threshold of 5% of GNI is determined by the Broadband Commission for Digital Development, jointly set up by the International Telecommunication Union (ITU) and the United Nations Educational, Scientific and Cultural Organization (UNESCO). Fixed-broadband prices refer to the prices of a monthly subscription to an entry-level fixed-broadband plan. Mobile-broadband prices refer to the prices of prepaid handset-based mobile-broadband plans with a data allowance of 500 MB per month.
Source: ITU (2016), *Measuring the Information Society Report 2016.*
StatLink https://doi.org/10.1787/888933800347

Transport infrastructure and logistics capabilities

Cross-border e-commerce allows people to do business on line, but it needs logistics to deliver traded physical goods. As a result, the growth of e-commerce is affected by not only trade costs, but also safety, security, reliability, transparency, flexibility and efficiency. E-commerce poses new challenges to storage, parcel delivery and express postal services. The development of e-commerce will require additional efforts in terms of both physical connectivity and trade-supporting services. Emerging Asia faces infrastructure obstacles such as the poor quality of roads, incomplete road and railway networks (Table 2.4).

Table 2.4. **Infrastructure quality in Emerging Asia**
Index, scale 1-7 from lowest to highest quality of infrastructure

Country	Quality of roads	Quality of railroad infrastructure	Quality of air transport infrastructure	Quality of port infrastructure	Quality of overall infrastructure
Brunei Darussalam	4.70	2.07	4.08	3.67	4.14
Cambodia	3.38	1.62	3.85	3.85	3.43
Indonesia	3.86	3.82	4.52	3.91	3.79
Lao PDR	3.42	n.a.	3.77	2.01	3.74
Malaysia	5.46	5.06	5.70	5.44	5.48
Myanmar	2.33	1.79	2.62	2.62	2.42
Philippines	3.07	1.97	3.25	2.92	3.04
Singapore	6.28	5.74	6.85	6.66	6.39
Thailand	4.21	2.52	4.95	4.18	4.03
Viet Nam	3.47	3.15	4.06	3.84	3.63
China	4.77	5.07	4.81	4.59	4.55
India	4.43	4.48	4.49	4.53	4.45
World	4.05	3.38	4.41	4.04	4.06

Notes: The score is based on the view of firm executives interviewed in the WEF (2017) *Executive Opinion Survey*. In landlocked countries, port infrastructure refers to access to seaports. Data for Myanmar are from 2015-16. Data for quality of railroad infrastructure in Brunei Darussalam are from 2012-13. n.a.= not available.
Source: WEF (2017), *Executive Opinion Survey*.

In terms of logistics, service is a key to the efficiency of distribution networks. The nature of e-commerce and demands of online consumers may motivate supply-chain operations to focus increasingly on near-sourcing, omni-channel and faster transport solutions (Inbound Logistics, 2014). A logistics network will be optimised only when it contains high-standard services, especially in some critical facilities in supply chains, such as mega e-fulfilment centres, parcel-sorting centres (hubs), local parcel distribution centres for last-mile supply chains, local city logistics depots and returns centres.

E-commerce payment systems

Payment systems – either online or offline – are vital components of e-commerce. Various solutions are available, including cash on delivery (CoD), prepaid, credit cards, debit cards, e-banking, mobile payment, smartcard and e-wallets, among others. Where available, a variety of options promotes e-commerce growth because it allows consumers to choose their preferred ways to pay for online business.

CoD remains the preferred payment method in many Emerging Asian countries, especially those in Southeast Asia. CoD is the predominant payment method for retail goods in India, Indonesia, the Philippines and Viet Nam for instance (Adyen, 2015; IFC, 2014). A firm survey found that in Viet Nam CoD accounts for more than 70% of payments to the surveyed companies (IFC, 2014). While CoD has its advantages in e-commerce trade such as payment security, it may be a less viable option for transactions across borders. To develop cross-border e-commerce, governments should encourage electronic payment (e-payment) which processes money transfer on line, enhance their e-payment system to alleviate security concerns of consumers and sellers, and establish proper regulations for the use of various online payment methods. Once regulations are created, they should be harmonised regionally.

Online e-commerce platforms can collect and integrate information from various sources and provide service packages to users. Reliable transaction credit systems help to strengthen trust given by participants and would create better business opportunities. With the growth of e-payment, many financial institutions have found it profitable to provide fiduciary loans using Internet finance. E-commerce platforms like eBay have started to launch cross-border insurance products to facilitate transactions.

Ideally, e-commerce development would be fostered by the building of a payment system that can accommodate existing market solutions and remain open to new approaches in the future. Rather than simply a payment network, the e-commerce payment system should also be part of a service platform that can ensure transition security, trace credit records and offer consumer protection. Security, privacy, creditability, reliability and efficiency are among the main factors to be considered. Building and maintaining the e-commerce payment system requires resources in terms of capital, technology and people. This will be a big challenge for those Emerging Asian countries whose domestic banking and financial systems are still at an early stage of development. At the same time, digital technologies and innovations in finance also offer opportunities for improving financial access (Box 2.3).

Box 2.3. Innovation for financial inclusion

Relatively speaking, Asian countries' development in the banking and finance sector lags behind their achievements in other aspects of economic growth. Problems in this sector – such as the low coverage of the banking network, a pre-mature personal/household credit system and the lack of an efficient capital market – may hold back a country's economic development. The traditional approach to establishing a modern banking system (like the ones that developed countries have today) would take a long time.

The digital economy offers opportunities to accelerate financial inclusion in developing countries with new technologies that are transforming the financial services landscape. Some of the notable examples include alternative platforms, such as mobile phones and digital platforms, to enable last-mile access; alternative digital information, such as biometrics data, to verify customer identity for account opening and payment authorisation; big data, such as transactional and digital footprint data, to improve customer targeting and credit risk assessment; and electronic money (e-money) to improve customer experience in savings and payments. These solutions can either complement the traditional banking and financial architecture, or be used independently. These new models are so efficient that even traditional financial service providers have become eager to adopt them.

In China, the digital economy has become an important contributor to a more inclusive financial system. Supported by rapid economic growth, online shopping and mobile payment are increasingly popular. As a result, digital finance is growing and supplementing the traditional financial system. For example, hundreds of millions of people are using third party online payment platforms such as AliPay and TenPay for daily transactions and their ease of usage helps bring basic financial services to small towns and villages. Small businesses have benefited from this trend as well, through peer-to-peer (P2P) lending by Fintech companies such as Ant Financial. Unlike traditional commercial banks, these digital finance companies use sophisticated models with Big Data to assess the risks of small borrowers and are able to provide funds to MSMEs that are usually left out of the traditional financial system.

> **Box 2.3. Innovation for financial inclusion** *(cont.)*
>
> New technologies can help to expand access to financial services in lower-income countries in the region as well. While about 80% of Cambodia's population live in rural areas and money transfer between rural and urban population is very common, fewer than 20% of Cambodian adults have access to financial services (Duflos, 2014). This forces many to resort to informal transfers which can be slow and risky. Digital finance helps address this challenge. Launched in 2009, Wing Limited Specialised Bank is the market leader for mobile banking services with one million users and provides an easy way for Cambodians, including the unbanked and under-banked, to make domestic money transfers, phone top-ups and bill payments. Many traditional micro-finance institutions have also followed the digital trend. For example, ACLEDA Bank and AMK Microfinance Institution, two largest of their kind in Cambodia, have launched mobile banking products in 2013 and early 2012 respectively.
>
> Viet Nam is another country in Southeast Asia with good potential for utilising digital technology to achieve financial inclusion, thanks to its increasingly robust ICT infrastructure and Internet penetration. Some companies have recognised and started to take advantage of this in recent years. For example, MoMo, a Fintech start-up launched in 2014, has amassed 2.5 million customers with its mobile wallet, e-payment and online banking services, becoming a market leader.
>
> These new opportunities in financial innovation also pose new challenges for regulators, however. The central bank of Indonesia introduced e-money regulations in 2009 and launched a follow-up Digital Financial Services pilot project four years later. In March 2015, the Financial Services Authority (OJK) introduced a nation-wide initiative called Laku Pandai to promote branchless banking and increase financial service penetration in remote regions. Significant progress has been made through these initiatives to target financially excluded, especially those in rural areas (ADB, 2017).

Legal and regulatory environment

The development of e-commerce requires new rules and regulations to improve trust, security and facility in the online marketplace. Without the necessary regulations, online commerce risks creating "grey" zones of international trade associated with problems such as tax evasion, fake products and violations of IPRs. When it comes to having the necessary regulatory infrastructure to support the digital economy, much of Emerging Asia generally performs well (Table 2.5). With the exception of Cambodia, all of the countries had an electronic transactions law by 2013, and Cambodia has prepared draft legislation in this regard. When it comes to the realm of privacy and data protection, however, performance varies more widely across the countries in Emerging Asia. Seven of the twelve countries already had a law covering these domains, and one further country was at the draft stage of legislation. Cambodia and Lao PDR had both prepared draft laws covering consumer protection. Cambodia and Lao PDR also lack laws on cybercrime, and content regulation laws were enacted in all countries in the region but Cambodia and the Philippines.

Table 2.5. **E-commerce laws in ASEAN Member States, 2013**

Country	Electronic transactions	Privacy	Cybercrime	Consumer protection	Content regulation	Domain names
Brunei Darussalam	Enacted	n.a.	Enacted	Partial	Enacted	Enacted
Cambodia	Draft	n.a.	Draft	n.a.	Draft	Enacted
Indonesia	Enacted	Partial	Enacted	Partial	Enacted	Enacted
Lao PDR	Enacted	n.a.	n.a.	Draft	Enacted	Partial
Malaysia	Enacted	Enacted	Enacted	Enacted	Enacted	Enacted
Myanmar	Enacted	n.a.	Enacted	Enacted	Enacted	Enacted
Philippines	Enacted	Enacted	Enacted	Enacted	n.a.	Enacted
Singapore	Enacted	Enacted	Enacted	Enacted	Enacted	Enacted
Thailand	Enacted	Partial	Enacted	Enacted	Partial	Partial
Viet Nam	Enacted	Partial	Enacted	Enacted	Enacted	Enacted

Source: UNCTAD (2013), *Review of E-commerce Legislation Harmonization in the Association of Southeast Asian Nations.*

A fair and competitive regulatory environment is needed to foster e-commerce activities. Regulation of e-commerce in particular and other relevant policy areas can both be important. Intellectual property rights, for example, can be particularly important in e-commerce, in a number of ways. Digital transactions often involve the buying and selling of products and services based on intellectual property – software, networks and other systems that underpin e-commerce are forms of intellectual property – and businesses involved in e-commerce often hold much of their value in intellectual property.

Taxation is another important issue, which can be complicated by cross-border e-commerce. The OECD has worked on taxation and e-commerce since the 1998 Ottawa Conference on Electronic Commerce and the Ottawa Taxation Framework Conditions. These principles included a call for neutrality, stating that tax systems should seek to be neutral between forms of e-commerce and between conventional transactions and e-commerce (OECD, 2015a).

Some countries in the region are implementing or considering new rules for taxing e-commerce. In Thailand, for example, the Revenue Department is developing draft transfer pricing legislation to improve revenue collection from firms engaged in e-commerce. Foreign operators with a presence in the country would be liable for Thai taxes. In 2016, China introduced tax reforms that changed the tax treatment of goods bought on line from overseas sellers, from that of personal postal articles to imported goods subject to additional taxes.

Data protection, privacy and security against computer crime are critical issues for ensuring the protection of consumer interests and for maintaining the integrity of e-commerce systems. Businesses should take responsibility for ensuring that their practices are "lawful, transparent and fair, enable consumer participation and choice, and provide reasonable security safeguards" (OECD, 2016).

Effective consumer protection is instrumental in creating an efficient and competitive marketplace that can offer accurate information about products and prices, ensure the interests and welfare of consumers, and contribute to Emerging Asia's economic development. This is especially true for e-commerce, where buyers and sellers of products or services do not deal with each other in person and must rely more on trust between both parties. The rapid development of e-commerce in the region in recent years has led to the rise of many Internet-related problems, such as cyber-crime. According to a multimarket survey for assessing the impact of Internet scams in several Emerging Asian countries, 90% of surveyed Internet users are aware of the existence of Internet scams, while 40% have been victims (Figure 2.10).

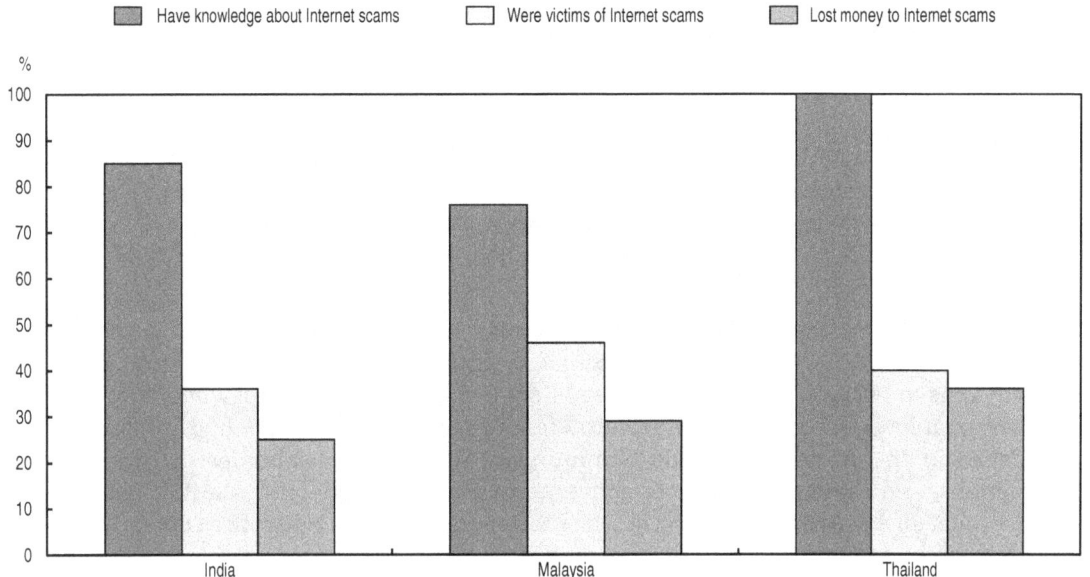

Figure 2.10. **Internet scams in selected Emerging Asian countries, 2016**
Percentage of surveyed population

Source: Telenor Group (2016), "Asia's Top Internet Scams and How to Stay Safe", www.telenor.com/asias-top-Internet-scams-and-how-to-stay-safe.
StatLink https://doi.org/10.1787/888933800366

The prevalence of cyber-crime and the lack of protection against it have become major barriers to the full release of Emerging Asia's e-commerce potential. Studies show that 58% of Southeast Asians are worried about sharing financial information on the Internet, especially those living in Indonesia, the Philippines and Malaysia, where high levels of fraud and cyber attacks exist (Google and Temasek, 2016). Low levels of trust in online transactions contribute to the preference for CoD payment in Southeast Asian countries, though offline payment methods like CoD increase risk and cost for merchants and hamper the growth of e-commerce (Nguyen, 2017). Electronic authentication systems are a useful tool for building confidence in e-commerce (Box 2.4).

Box 2.4. **Electronic authentication**

Electronic authentication is critical in verifying the identities of participants in digital transactions, which is needed to reduce uncertainty and build trust. The Ottawa Declaration on Authentication for Electronic Commerce adopted by OECD ministers at the October 1998 ministerial conference outlined plans for promoting the development and use of electronic authentication tools (OECD, 1998). In the time since, the OECD has carried out a number of initiatives to support the implementation of the Declaration, including developing the OECD Recommendation on Electronic Authentication and OECD Guidance for Electronic Authentication aims to support the improvement of electronic authentication systems, with a view to facilitating international co-operation on the issue. It recommends the establishment of technology-neutral approaches for domestic

> **Box 2.4. Electronic authentication** *(cont.)*
>
> and cross-border electronic authentication of persons and entities, fostering the development on new authentication products and services, encouraging cross-sectoral and cross-jurisdictional compatibility of authentication schemes, and increase awareness of the benefits of using authentication.
>
> As of 2012, there was some recognition of electronic signatures in all ASEAN member countries, according to a stocktaking exercise by UNCTAD. In Myanmar and Thailand, all legal signatures were recognised. In Brunei Darussalam, Indonesia, Lao PDR and Singapore, a two-tier approach was used where only advanced or qualified signatures were associated with legal presumptions. In the Philippines, Malaysia and Viet Nam, only signatures associated with a specific technology were recognised. None of the ten countries recognised only advanced or qualified signatures (UNCTAD, 2013).

In Southeast Asia, the ASEAN Strategic Action Plan for Consumer Protection (ASAPCP) 2016-25 sets out ASEAN's strategy for consumer policy over a ten-year period. The ASAPCP aims to establish a common ASEAN Consumer Protection Framework, ensure a high common level of consumer empowerment and protection, institute high consumer confidence in the ASEAN Economic Community (AEC) and cross-border commercial transactions, and integrate consumer concerns in all ASEAN policies. ASAPCP 2016-25 proposes that an ASEAN Regional Online Dispute Resolution (ODR) Network be established for cross-border complaints and investigations.

Policy challenges and conclusion

The potential of e-commerce has long been recognised, as has the need for the creation of a supportive policy environment for its growth. When OECD ministers concluded in 1998 that e-commerce would be the key engine for economic growth, e-commerce faced constraints in the areas of technology availability, consumer behaviours, and trade and services liberalisation. Two decades later, the market has matured to accommodate e-commerce growth, and progress in globalisation, trade liberalisation and regional integration has opened borders in global e-commerce. Most countries are including e-commerce and digital economy development in their national strategies and action plans (Box 2.5).

> **Box 2.5. E-commerce in national development plans**
>
> Expanding e-commerce for its own sake and to support policy goals is a priority in the medium-term national development plans of several Emerging Asian countries. The plans of countries such as Brunei Darussalam, Lao PDR and Thailand do not directly refer to e-commerce, but include targets for expanding Internet access and use by individuals and businesses. The Eleventh Malaysia Plan (2016-20) mentions e-commerce in several chapters: the e-payment platform for micro enterprises will be expanded, technology deployment in the logistics chain aims to support e-commerce activities, and e-commerce is one element of the development strategy outlined for small and medium-sized enterprises in Sabah and Sarawak. The Philippines Development Plan 2017-22 calls for developing potential in digital trade and e-commerce to boost services exports in particular, and targets the creation of services-related statistics to improve

> **Box 2.5. E-commerce in national development plans** *(cont.)*
>
> implementation and monitoring. The legislative priorities outlined in Cambodia's National Strategic Development Plan 2014-18 include promoting the adoption of the Law on Telecommunication and related laws for the sector, including e-commerce. The plan also calls for improved service and reduced fees by the Ministry of Post and Telecommunications through reforms that include the study of postal service and e-commerce.
>
> China's 13th Five-Year Plan incorporates e-commerce development in targets for several sectors. E-commerce is noted as a tool in promoting an "intelligent" agricultural sector, in facilitating new forms of trade for a "robust business environment" and in helping to develop "cross-Strait economic integration". Under the topic of strengthening information security, the plan targets e-commerce development in China by building relevant infrastructure, promoting innovation and adoption of these tools and practices, and establishing "international e-commerce thoroughfares" in experimental zones in Hangzhou and other areas. E-commerce is not discussed as prominently in India's Twelfth Five-Year Plan (2012-17), in which the issue is mentioned directly only in the context of reforms planned for India Post. The plan does, however, also refer to the need to adapt to digitalisation and to adopt ICT tools in economic activities more generally.

Governments have important roles to play in facilitating the growth of an e-commerce sector that benefits growth and development. Among the most important policy areas to be addressed are improvements in connectivity, development of digital skills and provision of digital security. To be effective, regional co-operation is needed across a number of policy areas.

Connectivity

To improve connectivity in terms of reach and quality, governments should strive for a multi-stakeholder approach to infrastructure development, broader regional co-operation and more vibrant market competition. The public sector should take the lead in infrastructure building, but it will need the private sector's involvement to make the development sustainable. Public-private partnerships, inter-governmental co-operation and foreign investment should be encouraged.

In addition to investing in physical infrastructure, improving the quality of related services directly affects the quality of connectivity. This is important particularly in cross-border e-commerce. Typically, logistics integrators play a crucial role in the distribution network of cross-border e-commerce, as they bring together online and offline supply chains of different countries. Even with well-constructed infrastructure, connectivity cannot function well without quality services. Governments should strengthen market competition to help improve the quality of services and reduce the cost of Internet connection. One reason for high-price, low-quality Internet connections in some Emerging Asian countries is the monopolistic power of a few telecommunication giants.

The emergence of new service intermediaries can lead to structural changes in commerce. E-commerce development generates more business opportunities for companies in areas such as material suppliers, market investigation, software development, shipment and delivery, agency operation, and the search for keywords and optimisation. As production networks clustering around core e-commerce companies start to deepen and spread out, this leads to a finer division of labour and therefore to higher specialisation. With market segmentation, demand is more precisely identified, and therefore service activities can expand. In this way, the growth of services can be market-driven.

It is worth noting that Emerging Asian economies are facing challenges from development gaps existing both within countries, especially between metropolitan and remote rural areas, and between countries. Enhancing regional co-operation can help in providing solutions to these challenges. This is in particular helpful for those countries that are facing big obstacles from capacity and resource limits and capital or technology. Some recent developments include China's Belt and Road initiative, Japan's USD 110 billion proposal on infrastructure in ASEAN, and the establishment of the Asian Infrastructure Investment Bank (AIIB).

Skills and human capital development

Emerging Asia has considerable human resource potential. The total population of ASEAN, China and India reached 3.3 billion by the end of 2015, with 70% of the population aged between 15 and 64; this represents a huge consumer market and labour force. The number of people with Internet access increased from less than 60 million in 2001 to more than 1.2 billion in 2015. Speakers of regional languages – particularly Chinese, Indonesians and Malaysians – are among the most numerous Internet users in the world. Developing this potential is increasingly important: the International Labour Organization (ILO) concludes that by the end of 2012, knowledge-based jobs absorbed more than 7% of China's workforce. In ASEAN, knowledge-intensive activities created an estimated 42 million jobs in 2012; in 2016, more than 51 million employees were taking knowledge-intensive jobs, representing more than 13% of the region's total workforce (ILO, 2016).

Digital skills have played a critical role in driving the adoption of new technologies and the skills challenge has serious implications for e-commerce development in Emerging Asia. First, e-commerce is knowledge-intensive. High-tech devices, software and applications are widely used in production and business. Qualified labour must have sufficient technical skills to handle these tools proficiently, especially for problem-solving. Second, with ICT and service-sector development, the global value chains behind e-commerce are much more sophisticated than ever before. High managerial skills are needed to operate the network and monitor its functioning. Third, with the rapid growth of B2C and C2C e-commerce, users now have skills that once belonged only to experts; these include knowing about home and overseas markets, understanding different consumer habits and learning trading rules. Fourth, participants in e-commerce must be able to learn quickly about new technologies and business models that continuously emerge in the market. Fifth, innovation is a key to competitiveness. Reliance on homogenous products or services cannot lead to long-term success in e-commerce. The most innovative elements or stages usually create the most added value from GVCs.

Governments will need to give priority to improving digital literacy. Many Emerging Asian countries lack digital literacy, and this negatively affects Internet penetration. Digital literacy is defined as the set of competencies required for full participation in a knowledge society; these include skills for effective use of digital devices such as smartphones, tablets, laptops and desktop PCs. Improving digital literacy could help boost digital awareness and prepare the population for engaging in e-commerce. Improved worker and management skills could help smaller firms to increase their participation in cross-border e-commerce and to join global value chains. In Asia, SMEs account for more than 95% of all enterprises and employ more than 80% of the workforce. E-commerce development and the expansion of GVCs and related services help SMEs get involved in GVCs and better benefit from globalisation. This helps SMEs access information, explore new markets and obtain financing, and enhances the links among suppliers, producers and consumers

Improvements can be made by including digital literacy courses in educational curricula, providing sufficient equipment such as computers to schools to implement these courses, and offering training to adults. The region's education lags behind that of developed countries. While the problem of education is not specific to e-commerce, rapid e-commerce growth and the desire to grasp development opportunities associated with economic digitalisation have spurred developing countries to accelerate improvements in education, which is supposed to be a long-term project. Reforms may be needed that target access to and quality of education.

Increasing students' access to computers will help develop needed skills. Of the eight jurisdictions in Emerging Asia included in the OECD's 2012 Programme for International Student Assessment (PISA) survey (OECD, 2015b), a majority of students had access to at least one home computer in all jurisdictions except Indonesia and Viet Nam; only 25.8% of students in Indonesia and 38.9% in Viet Nam had access to a home computer (Figure 2.11). All or nearly all students had access to a home computer in Hong Kong, China (100%); Macau, China (99.4%); Singapore (96.9%); and Shanghai, China (91.9%). The increase in home computer access from 2009 to 2012 was greatest in Malaysia (10.6%); Shanghai, China (10.2%); and Thailand (10.1%). Computers were relatively more available in schools in the three Chinese jurisdictions, Singapore and Thailand, all of which had 3.1 or fewer students sharing each computer; these numbers are below the OECD average of 4.7. In Viet Nam, there were 8.6 students per computer, while Indonesia had 16.4 and Malaysia 16.7. To be effective learning tools in the classroom and at home, computers need to be connected to the Internet and used in a way that complements and does not distract from learning.

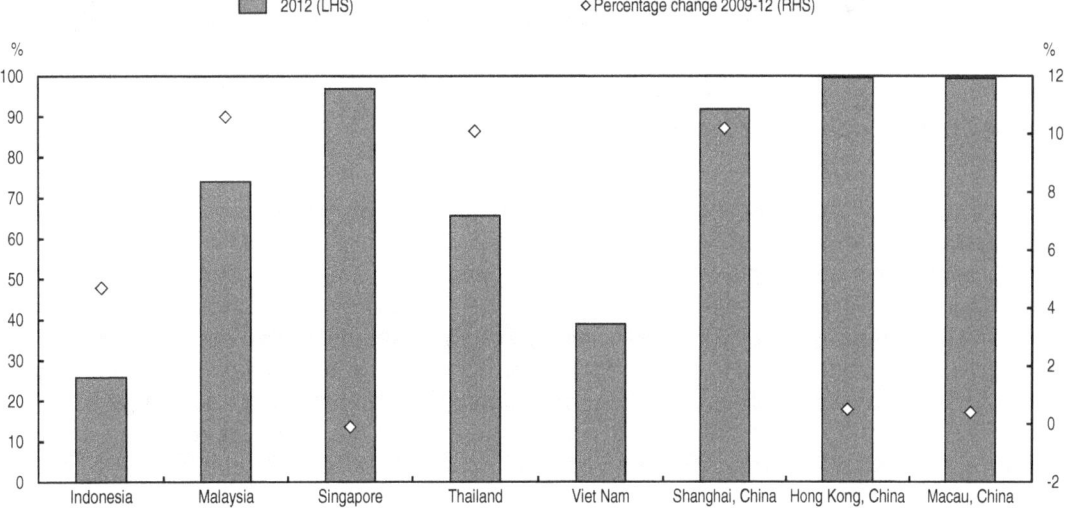

Figure 2.11. **Students with at least one computer at home, 2009-12**

Note: Percentage change in 2009-12 is not available for Viet Nam.
Source: OECD (2015b), PISA 2012 Database, www.oecd.org/pisa/pisaproducts/pisa2012database-downloadabledata.htm.
StatLink https://doi.org/10.1787/888933799644

Another aspect of the skills challenge concerns the free movement of skilled labour, which helps to diffuse knowledge. Labour mobility across countries in Emerging Asia faces barriers: the non-recognition of academic diplomas and professional certificates, the lack of information about labour market opportunities and domestic restrictions on work permission for foreigners.

Digital security and consumer protection

Governments will need to support e-commerce development by providing a more secure cyberspace. Cross-border e-commerce often involves buyers and sellers located in different countries, governed by different laws and regulations, and using different currencies and possibly different languages. Given the added complexity, it becomes more difficult to protect consumers' rights in cross-border e-commerce, compared with domestic e-commerce.

Countries will need to provide their consumer protection enforcement agencies with the authority to investigate, pursue, obtain and, where appropriate, share relevant information and evidence, particularly on matters relating to cross-border fraudulent and deceptive commercial practices. That authority should extend to co-operation with foreign consumer-protection enforcement agencies and other appropriate foreign counterparts (OECD, 2016).

In addition to regional co-operation, domestic legal support is also important. Many countries in Emerging Asia still have no national legislation to support cross-border e-commerce (ADBI, 2016); when disputes occur, the legal system has to rely on the existing law which may not be the most suitable. For example, in 2015 a consumer in China filed a lawsuit against a cross-border e-commerce company for not properly labelling the foreign product it was selling. The lawsuit was rejected because the court considered the relationship between the consumer and the e-commerce company as between client and proxy agent, instead of between buyer and seller. Under the current legal system in China, cross-border e-commerce companies do not bear any legal responsibility as sellers (SDAIC, 2017). If not addressed, the lack of legal protection will likely discourage consumers from making cross-border transactions and weaken their trust in cross-border e-commerce.

Last but not least, governments should increase information sharing about the risks associated with cross-border e-commerce by creating dedicated websites and establishing comprehensive databases so that both consumers and businesses can be informed about the challenges they face and prepare for them accordingly.

Regional and international co-operation

International co-operation is important across multiple policy areas related to e-commerce. Governments should harmonise regulatory frameworks to facilitate the development of cross-border e-commerce, as cross-border e-commerce development promotes the formation of global governance on digital trade. Rule setting in international information flow is one example. Information is the lifeblood of e-commerce, extensively affecting the economy, society and even national security. It may be challenging, however, to keep a balance between the free movement of information and data/privacy protection. While insufficient regulations will not be able to ensure market fairness and competition, excessive restriction – particularly when implemented for protectionist reasons – may negatively affect the free movement and accuracy of data. Effective solutions will help strengthen security and IPR protection, as well as contribute to trust and legislation, therefore promoting e-commerce in the long run.

Moreover, when e-commerce involves buyers and sellers in different countries, transactions are subjected to almost all issues that apply to other forms of trade. Accordingly, countries interested in promoting cross-border e-commerce should adopt policies in favour of globalisation and trade facilitation by removing tariff or non-tariff barriers and simplifying customs, inspection and taxation procedures, etc. Cross-border e-commerce often finds difficulties in customs clearance, exchange settlement and tax reimbursement, especially for small-volume trade flows. The World Economic Forum estimates that lowering the supply-chain barriers, such as customs formalities, between countries would increase cross-border e-commerce by 60% to 80% (WEF, 2013).

Regulations on e-commerce will cover traditional trade issues (including tariffs and non-tariff measures, trade facilitation, and protection of IPRs) as well as new issues (including cross-border information flows, privacy protection, data localisation and source codes disclosure). Although many countries have agreed on trade facilitation issues, such as the acceptance of electronic authentication in commercial transactions and the use of customised electronic formats in paperless trade, it is not easy to reach an agreement on some other core issues about e-commerce. In principle, Emerging Asian countries will benefit from collaboration in the region-wide e-commerce enabling environment, such as the 2000 e-ASEAN Framework Agreement which outlined regional plans to develop the ICT sector, reduce the digital divide within and among member states, promote co-operation between the public and private sectors, and promote liberalisation of trade in relevant goods and services as well as investment. Thanks to the progress of regional integration, leaders can now discuss these issues at the ASEAN Economic Ministers' meetings, East Asian Summit, and ASEAN Plus One dialogues/meetings.

A range of policy areas related to e-commerce have been addressed at the regional level. For instance, an ASEAN Agreement on E-commerce is currently being discussed by ASEAN Member States and it is set to be finalised by the end of 2018. The Agreement aims to streamline regional trade rules governing e-commerce to promote greater digital connectivity and lower operating barriers to entry for businesses (MTI, 2018). The establishment of ASEAN Agreement on E-commerce is a key element of ASEAN Work Programme on Electronic Commerce (AWPEC) 2017-2025 based on AEC Blueprint 2025. Within the next decade, the AWPEC will facilitate cross-border e-commerce in ASEAN by raising multi-sectoral initiatives in the areas of infrastructure, education and technology competency, consumer protection, modernisation of the legal framework, security of electronic transactions, payment systems, trade facilitation, competition, and logistics (ASEAN, 2017).

Multilateral trade negotiation seems to provide an ideal platform for developing countries to participate in global rule-settings on e-commerce. However, partially because of the WTO stalemate, in reality most issues about e-commerce are addressed mainly in bilateral free-trade agreements and regional initiatives. For instance, the ASEAN-Australia Digital Trade Standards Initiative aims at developing and using international standards that will remove barriers and promote digital trade. In addition, progress in multilateral trade negotiations can hardly catch up with the rapid growth of e-commerce. The so-called 21st century free-trade agreements (FTAs containing WTO-plus and WTO-extra provisions) tend to be pilots in new rule-making. Emerging Asian countries are among the world's most populous and fastest-growing market for e-commerce, and they should remain active in the new rule-making. Moreover, by first harmonising the region's e-commerce-related regulations, countries in the region can act as a group to ensure its voice on global rule settings on e-commerce governance is heard.

Cross-border e-commerce is one of the major development trends of international trade and globalisation. The development of e-commerce provides new opportunities to help Emerging Asian countries reduce poverty, narrow inequality and avoid the middle-income trap. Emerging Asian countries have advantages from their capacities in technology adoption and incremental innovation. However, to better grasp the opportunities for growth, they need to make progress in connectivity, skills development, rules and regulations and other areas.

Notes

1. By definition, knowledge-intensive jobs include the following ISCO-08 categories: 1) managers; 2) professionals; and 3) technicians and associate professionals.
2. Here the aggregate data of ASEAN does not include Lao PDR and Myanmar because of the lack of data for these two countries.
3. In 1998, the WTO Ministerial Conference adopted the Declaration on Global Electronic Commerce aiming to establish a comprehensive work programme to examine all trade-related issues concerning global electronic commerce, but there was no substantive progress afterward.

References

Adyen (2015), *The Global E-Commerce Payments Guide*, https://www.adyen.com/blog/the-global-e-commerce-payments-guide.

ADB (2017), *Accelerating financial inclusion in South-East Asia with digital finance*, Asian Development Bank, Manila, https://www.adb.org/sites/default/files/publication/222061/financial-inclusion-se-asia.pdf.

ADBI (2016), "The Development Dimension of E-Commerce in Asia: Opportunities and Challenges", Asian Development Bank Institute, Tokyo, https://www.adb.org/sites/default/files/publication/185050/adbi-pb2016-2.pdf.

Akamai (2017), *State of the Internet Connectivity Report*, www.akamai.com/fr/fr/multimedia/documents/state-of-the-Internet/q1-2017-state-of-the-Internet-connectivity-report.pdf (accessed 24 August 2017).

ASEAN (2017), "ASEAN Work Programme on Electronic Commerce 2017-2025", Association of Southeast Asian Nations, Jakarta, http://asean.org/asean-economic-community/sectoral-bodies-under-the-purview-of-aem/e-commerce/.

ASEAN (2000), *e-ASEAN Framework Agreement*, Association of Southeast Asian Nations, Jakarta, http://asean.org/?static_post=e-asean-framework-agreement.

A.T. Kearney (2015), "Lifting the Barriers to E-Commerce in ASEAN", https://www.atkearney.co.uk/documents/10192/5540871/Lifting+the+Barriers+to+E-Commerce+in+ASEAN.pdf.

BCG (2014), *Cross-border E-commerce Makes the World Flatter*, The Boston Consulting Group, Boston, https://www.bcg.com/perspectives/170622.

Duflos, E. (2014), *Financial Inclusion in Cambodia is Trending Digital*, The Consultative Group to Assist the Poor, Washington, DC, http://www.cgap.org/blog/financial-inclusion-cambodia-trending-digital.

eMarketer (2016), *Mobile and Internet Usage Propels Southeast Asia's Retail Ecommerce Sector*, https://www.emarketer.com/Article/Mobile-Internet-Usage-Propels-Southeast-Asias-Retail-Ecommerce-Sector/1014431.

Google and Temasek (2016), "E-conomy SEA: unlocking the $200 billion digital opportunity in Southeast Asia", https://www.slideshare.net/economySEA/economy-sea-by-google-and-temasek.

IFC (2014), *E- and M-Commerce and Payment Sector Development in Vietnam*, International Finance Corporation, Washington, DC.

ILO (2016), *ASEAN in Transformation*, International Labour Organization, Geneva, http://www.ilo.org/public/english/dialogue/actemp/downloads/publications/2016/asean_in_transf_2016_r3_persp.pdf.

Inbound Logistics (2014), "Adapting your supply chain for the future…now", www.inboundlogistics.com/cms/article/adapting-your-supply-chain-for-the-futurenow/ (accessed 30 August 2017).

ITU (2016), *Measuring the Information Society Report 2016*, International Telecommunication Union, Geneva, https://www.itu.int/en/ITU-D/Statistics/Documents/publications/misr2016/MISR2016-w4.pdf.

MTI (2018), *ASEAN Agreement on Electronic Commerce*, Ministry of Trade and Industry, Singapore.

Ng, T.H., C.T. Lye and Y.S. Lim (2013), "Broadband penetration and economic growth in ASEAN countries: a generalized method of moments approach", *Applied Economics Letters*, Vol. 20/9, pp. 857–862.

OECD (2018), *Economic Outlook for Southeast Asia, China and India 2018: Fostering Growth through Digitalisation*, OECD Publishing, Paris. http://dx.doi.org/10.1787/9789264286184-en.

OECD (2016), *OECD Recommendation of the Council on Consumer Protection in E-Commerce*, OECD Publishing, Paris, http://dx.doi.org/10.1787/9789264255258-en.

OECD (2015a), *International VAT/GST Guidelines*, OECD Publishing, Paris, www.oecd.org/ctp/consumption/international-vat-gst-guidelines.pdf.

OECD (2015b), *PISA 2012 Database*, OECD Publishing, Paris, www.oecd.org/pisa/pisaproducts/pisa2012database-downloadabledata.htm (accessed 30 August 2017).

OECD (2000), *OECD Economic Outlook 67*, OECD Publishing, Paris, http://dx.doi.org/10.1787/data-00099-en.

OECD (1998), "OECD Ministerial Conference – A Borderless World: Realising the Potential of Global Electronic Commerce – Ottawa, Canada, 7-9 October 1998, Conference Conclusions", *OECD Publishing, Paris*, http://search.oecd.org/officialdocuments/displaydocumentpdf/?doclanguage=en&cote=sg/ec(98)14/final).

Nguyen, Q. (2017), "Cross-border B2C e-commerce in Southeast Asia: key trends and solutions", https://medium.com/fast-forward-advisors-blog/cross-border-b2c-e-commerce-in-southeast-asia-key-trends-and-solutions-bcf34cdae939.

SDAIC (2017), "Thoughts about cross-border e-commerce consumer protection, Shandong Administration for Industry and Commerce", Shandong Administration for Industry and Commerce, Jinan, http://www.sdaic.gov.cn/sdgsj/xwzx/gsdt/jyjl/911595/index.html.

Statista (2016), "Mobile shopping penetration worldwide as of March 2016, by region", www.statista.com/statistics/418393/mcommercepenetration-worldwide-region/ (accessed 30 August 2017).

Telenor Group (2016), "Asia's top Internet scams and how to stay safe", www.telenor.com/asias-top-Internet-scams-and-how-to-stay-safe (accessed 30 August 2017).

UNCTAD (2017), *UNCTADSTAT* (database), United Nations Conference on Trade and Development, Geneva, http://unctadstat.unctad.org.

UNCTAD (2013), *Review of E-commerce Legislation Harmonization in the Association of Southeast Asian Nations*, United Nations Conference on Trade and Development, Geneva, http://unctad.org/en/PublicationsLibrary/dtlstict2013d1_en.pdf.

UNDESA (2018), *UN E-Government Development Database*, United Nations Department of Economic and Social Affairs, New York, http://unpan3.un.org/egovkb/.

World Bank (2017), *World Development Indicators* (database), Washington, DC, http://data.worldbank.org/data-catalog/world-development-indicators.

WEF (2017), *Executive Opinion Survey*, World Economic Forum, Geneva.

WEF (2013), *Enabling Trade: Valuing Growth Opportunities*, World Economic Forum with Bain & Company and the World Bank, http://www3.weforum.org/docs/WEF_SCT_EnablingTrade_Report_2013.pdf.

Statistical annex

Table A.1. Real GDP growth of Southeast Asia, China and India
Annual percentage change

Country	2016	2017	2018	2019
ASEAN-5				
Indonesia	5.0	5.1	5.3	5.4
Malaysia	4.2	5.9	5.3	5.1
Philippines	6.9	6.7	6.7	6.7
Thailand	3.3	3.9	4.0	3.9
Viet Nam	6.2	6.8	6.9	6.6
Brunei Darussalam and Singapore				
Brunei Darussalam	-2.5	1.3	1.5	2.1
Singapore	2.4	3.6	3.5	3.0
CLM countries				
Cambodia	6.9	7.0	7.0	7.0
Lao PDR	7.0	6.9	6.8	6.9
Myanmar	5.9	6.8	6.9	7.1
China and India				
China	6.7	6.9	6.7	6.4
India	7.1	6.7	7.4	7.5
Average of ASEAN 10 countries	**4.8**	**5.3**	**5.3**	**5.3**
Average of Emerging Asia	**6.4**	**6.5**	**6.6**	**6.5**

Note: The cut-off date for data used is 18 June 2018. ASEAN and Emerging Asia growth rates are the weighted averages of the individual economies subsumed. Cambodia and Myanmar's 2017 data are preliminary estimates. The data for India and Myanmar follow fiscal years. For Myanmar, 2018 refers to the interim six-month period from April 2018 to September 2018, while 2019 refers to the fiscal year from October 2018 to September 2019. The projections for China, India and Indonesia are based on the OECD Economic Outlook No. 103 (database).
Source: OECD Development Centre, MPF-2018 (Medium-term Projection Framework).

Table A.2. Current account balances of Southeast Asia, China and India
Percentage of GDP

Country	2016	2017	2018	2019
ASEAN-5				
Indonesia	-1.8	-1.7	-1.8	-1.7
Malaysia	2.4	3.0	2.4	2.2
Philippines	-0.4	-0.8	-1.2	-1.4
Thailand	11.7	10.6	10.5	8.5
Viet Nam	3.0	2.9	2.9	2.8
Brunei Darussalam and Singapore				
Brunei Darussalam	15.5	19.0	10.5	10.0
Singapore	19.0	18.8	19.2	19.0
CLM countries				
Cambodia	-11.2	-10.9	-9.5	-9.2
Lao PDR	-14.1	-13.0	-9.3	-9.1
Myanmar	-4.0	-5.0	-5.2	-5.6
China and India				
China	1.8	1.4	1.2	1.2
India	-0.6	-1.9	-2.5	-2.7
Average of ASEAN 10 countries	**2.6**	**2.4**	**1.8**	**1.5**
Average of Emerging Asia	**1.4**	**0.8**	**0.5**	**0.3**

Note: The cut-off date for data used is 18 June 2018. The weighted averages are used for ASEAN average and Emerging Asia average. Data for India and Myanmar follow fiscal years. For Myanmar, 2018 refers to the interim 6-month period from April 2018 to September 2018 while 2019 refers to fiscal year starting October 2018 to September 2019. The projections for China, India and Indonesia are based on the OECD Economic Outlook No. 103 (database).
Source: OECD Development Centre, MPF-2018 (Medium-term Projection Framework); CEIC; country sources and ADB ADO April 2018.

Table A.3. **General government financial balances of Southeast Asia, China and India**
Percentage of GDP

Country	2018	2019
ASEAN-5		
Indonesia	-2.3	-2.2
Malaysia	-2.7	-2.6
Philippines	-1.9	-2.0
Thailand	-2.2	-2.3
Viet Nam	-5.9	-5.6
China and India		
China	-3.0	-3.2
India	-6.3	-6.0
ASEAN-5 average	**-2.4**	**-2.4**
Emerging Asia average	**-3.7**	**-3.7**

Note: The cut-off date for data used is 18 June 2018. Weighted averages are used for ASEAN average and Emerging Asia average. Data for India follow fiscal years. The projections for China, India and Indonesia are based on the OECD Economic Outlook No. 103 (database). General government balances data are not necessarily comparable to the budget balances published by national governments. Emerging Asia in this chart is comprised of ASEAN-5, China and India.

Source: OECD Development Centre, MPF-2018 (Medium-term Projection Framework).

ORGANISATION FOR ECONOMIC CO-OPERATION AND DEVELOPMENT

The OECD is a unique forum where governments work together to address the economic, social and environmental challenges of globalisation. The OECD is also at the forefront of efforts to understand and to help governments respond to new developments and concerns, such as corporate governance, the information economy and the challenges of an ageing population. The Organisation provides a setting where governments can compare policy experiences, seek answers to common problems, identify good practice and work to co-ordinate domestic and international policies.

The OECD member countries are: Australia, Austria, Belgium, Canada, Chile, the Czech Republic, Denmark, Estonia, Finland, France, Germany, Greece, Hungary, Iceland, Ireland, Israel, Italy, Japan, Korea, Latvia, Lithuania, Luxembourg, Mexico, the Netherlands, New Zealand, Norway, Poland, Portugal, the Slovak Republic, Slovenia, Spain, Sweden, Switzerland, Turkey, the United Kingdom and the United States. The European Union takes part in the work of the OECD.

OECD Publishing disseminates widely the results of the Organisation's statistics gathering and research on economic, social and environmental issues, as well as the conventions, guidelines and standards agreed by its members.

OECD DEVELOPMENT CENTRE

The Development Centre of the Organisation for Economic Co-operation and Development was established in 1962 and comprises 27 member countries of the OECD: Belgium, Chile, the Czech Republic, Denmark, Finland, France, Germany, Greece, Iceland, Ireland, Israel, Italy, Japan, Korea, Luxembourg, Mexico, the Netherlands, Norway, Poland, Portugal, Slovak Republic, Slovenia, Spain, Sweden, Switzerland, Turkey and the United Kingdom. In addition, 25 non-OECD countries are full members of the Development Centre: Brazil (since March 1994); India (February 2001); Romania (October 2004); Thailand (March 2005); South Africa (May 2006); Egypt and Viet Nam (March 2008); Colombia (July 2008); Indonesia (February 2009); Costa Rica, Mauritius, Morocco and Peru (March 2009); the Dominican Republic (November 2009); Senegal (February 2011); Argentina and Cabo Verde (March 2011); Panama (July 2013); Côte d'Ivoire, Kazakhstan and Tunisia (January 2015); the People's Republic of China (July 2015), Ghana and Uruguay (October 2015) and Paraguay (March 2017). The European Union also takes part in the work of the Centre.

The Development Centre occupies a unique place within the OECD and in the international community. It provides a platform where developing and emerging economies interact on an equal footing with OECD members to promote knowledge sharing and peer learning on sustainable and inclusive development. The Centre combines multidisciplinary analysis with policy dialogue activities to help governments formulate innovative policy solutions to the global challenges of development. Hence, the Centre plays a key role in the OECD's engagement efforts with non-member countries.

To increase the impact and legitimacy of its work, the Centre adopts an inclusive approach and engages with a variety of governmental and non-governmental stakeholders. It works closely with experts and institutions from its member countries, has established partnerships with key international and regional organisations and hosts networks of private-sector enterprises, think tanks and foundations working for development. The results of its work are discussed in experts' meetings as well as in policy dialogues and high-level meetings, and are published in a range of high-quality publications and papers for the research and policy communities.

For more information on the Centre, please see *www.oecd.org/dev*.